DYNAMIC THOUGHT

OR THE LAW OF VIBRANT ENERGY

WILLIAM WALKER ATKINSON

TRUE SIGN
PUBLISHING HOUSE

Published by True Sign Publishing House
Address: SY. No. 21/2 & 21/3, Sonnenahalli,
Krishnarajapura, Bengaluru,
Karnataka - 560049 India
E-mail: truesignbooks@gmail.com
Website: www.truesign.in

Dynamic Thought
Or The Law of Vibrant Energy
Author: William Walker Atkinson

ISBN: 978-93-5584-014-1

First Edition: 2022

Contents

"I am attacked by two very opposite sects—the Scientists and the Know-Nothngs; both laugh at me, calling me the 'Frogs' Dancing Master,' but I know that I have discovered one of the greatest Forces in Nature."

—GALVINI.

A Foreword

This is a queer book. It is a marriage of the Ancient Occult Teachings to the latest and most advanced conceptions of Modern Science—an odd union, for the parties thereto are of entirely different temperaments. The marriage might be expected to result disastrously, were it not for the fact that a connecting link has been found that gives them a bond of common interest. No two people may truly love each other, unless they also love something in common—the more they love in common, the greater will be their love for each other. And, let us trust that this will prove true in this marriage of Occultism and Science, celebrated in this book.

The Occultists usually get at the "facts," first, but they manage to evolve such outrageous theories to explain the facts, that the world will have none of their wares, and turns to Science for something "reasonable." Science, proceeding along different lines, at first denies these "facts" of the Occultists, not finding them accounted for by any of her existing theories; but, later on, when the "facts" have been finally thrust under her eyes, after repeated attempts and failures, she says, "Oh, yes, of course!" and proceeds to evolve a new theory, welding it with other scientific hypotheses, and after attaching a new label thereto, she proudly exhibits the thing as "the latest discovery of Modern Science"—and smiles indulgently, or indignantly, when the theory of the old Occultists is mentioned, saying, "Quite a different thing, we assure you!" And yet, in all justice, be it said, Science usually proceeds to find much better "proofs" to fit the "facts" of Occultism, than did the Occultists themselves. The Occultist "sees things," but is a poor hand at "proofs"—while the Scientist is great on "proofs," but so often, and so long, fails to see many things patent to the Occultist who is able to "look within" himself, but who is then unable to positively and scientifically "prove" the facts. This is easily explained—the Occultist's information comes from "within," while the Scientist's comes from without—and "proofs" belong to the "without" side of Mentation. And this is why the Occultists so often make such a bungle regarding "proofs" and the Scientist fails to see "facts" that are staring the Occultist in the face.

The whole history of Occultism and Science proves the above. Take the phenomenon called "Mesmerism" for instance—it was an old story with the Occultists, who had been for years aware of it, theoretically and practically. Mesmer brought it into general prominence, and Science laughed at it and at Mesmer's "fluid" theory, and called him a charlatan and imposter. Years afterwards, Braid, an English surgeon, discovered that some of the facts of "Mesmerism" were true, and he announced his discovery in a scientific manner, and lo! his views were accepted, and the thing was called "Hypnotism," poor old Mesmer being forgotten, because of his theory. Then, after a number of years, certain other aspects of the phenomenon were discovered, and scientifically relabelled "Suggestion," and the re-naming was supposed to "explain" the entire subject, the learned ones now saying, "Pooh, 'tis nothing but 'Suggestion,'" as if *that* explained the matter. But so far, they have only accepted certain phases of this form of Dynamic Thought—for that is what it is, and there are many other phases of which they do not dream.

And the same is true of the Occult Teaching that there is "Life in Everything—the Universe is Alive." For years, this idea was hooted at, and we had learned scientific discourses upon "dead Matter," "inert substance," etc. But, only within the past decade—yes, within the last five years, has Science discovered that there was Life in Everything, and that even in the Atom of mineral and chemical substance, there was to be found evidence of Mind. And Science is beginning to plume itself on its "recent discovery," and to account for it by a new theory, which is "quite a different thing, we assure you," from the old Occult Theory.

And the same will prove true in the case of the Occult Teaching of an Universal Mind, or Cosmic Mind. Science and Philosophy have long laughed at this, but even now their foremost investigators have come to the borders of a new country, and are gasping in amazement at what they see beyond its borders—they are now talking about "Life and Mind in the Ether"—and before long they will discard their paradoxical, absurd, hypothetical Ether, and say, "We are bathed in an Ocean of Mind"—only they will insist that this "Ocean of Mind" is, somehow, a "secretion of Matter"—something oozing out from the pores of Matter, perhaps.

But Science is doing valuable work in the direction of investigation and experiment, and in this way is *proving the principal occult teachings* in a way impossible to the Occultists themselves.

So, you see that both Occultism and Science have their own work to do—and neither can do the work of the other. Just now Science is coquetting with the question of "Thought Transmission," etc., at which she has for so long sneered and laughed. By and by she will accept the facts, and then proceed to prove them by a series of careful and conclusive experiments, and will then announce the result, solemnly, as "a triumph of Science."

And so, in this book you will find a marriage of the old Occult Teachings and Modern Scientific Researches and Investigation. And the two are bound together with that bond forged by the writer of the book—heated in the oven of his mind, and hammered into shape with his "untrained" thought—a crude, clumsy thing, but it serves its purpose—a thing called "*The Theory of Dynamic Thought*."

And so, this is what this Theory is—a "*tie that binds*." How you will like it depends upon yourself. For himself, the writer does not hesitate to say that he is pleased with his handiwork, rude, and clumsy though it may be. He believes that he has made a thing that will stand wear and tear, and that though it be not beautifully finished, it "will serve," and "be useful." And that is the main thing, after all. And, then, perhaps, some may see beauty in the very crudeness of the thing—may see that it bears the loving mark of the hammer that beat it into shape—may recognize that over it has passed the caress of the hand that made it—and in that seeing there may come the recognition of a beauty that is beyond "prettiness."

WILLIAM WALKER ATKINSON.

Los Angeles, California,
February 16, 1906.

"A fire-mist and a planet,
A crystal and a cell,
A jelly-fish and a saurian,
And caves where the cave-men dwell;
Then a sense of law and beauty,
And a face turned from the clod,—
Some call it Evolution,
And others call it God."
"Like tides on a crescent sea-beach,
When the moon is new and thin,
Into our hearts high yearnings
Come welling and surging in,—
Come from the mystic ocean
Whose rim no foot has trod,—
Some of us call it Longing,
And others call it God."

—W.H. Carruth.

CHAPTER-I
"In The Beginning"

THIS book will deal with Life. It holds that Life is Universal—that it is inherent in, and manifests (in different degrees) in every part, particle, phase, aspect, condition, place, or relationship, in the World of Things that we call the Universe.

It holds that Life manifests in two aspects or forms, which are generally found by us in connection and co-operation with each other, but which are both, probably, an expression of some One Thing higher than either. These two aspects or forms, which together go to make up or produce that which we know as "Life," are known as (1) Substance or Matter; and (2) Mind. In this book the term "Substance" is used in preference to "Matter," owing to the fact that the term "Matter" has become closely identified with certain ideas of the Materialistic school of thought, and has generally been regarded by the public in the light of "dead matter," whereas this book holds that all Substance is Alive. The term "Mind" is used in the sense of "Mind, *as we know it*," rather than as "Mind, *as it is*"—or, as "The Cosmic Mind." In some places the term "Mind-principle" is used to convey the idea of "a portion of the Great Principle of Mind, of which that which we call 'Mind' is but a small and but partially expressed portion." These terms are explained and illustrated as we proceed. The aspect of "Energy or Force" is not treated as a separate aspect or form of Life, in this book, for the reason that it is regarded as merely a manifestation of Mind, as will appear as we proceed. We have much to say regarding Motion, but the writer has tried to explain and prove that, at the last, all Motion results from Mental Action, and that all Force and Energy is Vital-Mental Force and Energy.

This book is not intended to run along metaphysical or theological lines—its field is different. And so, while it recognizes the importance of these branches of human thought, still, it finds that its own particular field is sufficient to engross its entire attention, for the moment, and, consequently the aforesaid subjects shall not be touched upon except incidentally, in connection with the subject matter of the book.

This being the case, there will be no discussion of the "origin of Life"—the question of "creation"—the problems of theology and metaphysics—the riddle of the "Why and Wherefore" of Life and the Universe. The writer has his own opinions upon these questions, but feels that this is not the place in which to air the same. For the purposes of the book, he prefers to leave every reader to his own favorite views and conceptions regarding these great subjects, feeling that the views regarding Life, Mind, Motion and Substance, that are advanced in this book, may be accepted by any intelligent reader, without prejudice to his, or her, accepted religious or philosophical views.

The writer sees that this something called "Life" exists—he finds it in evidence everywhere. And he sees it always in its aspects of Substance and Mind. And he feels justified in regarding "Life" as always existing in, and manifesting in these aspects—always in conjunction—at least, Life "as we know it."

And he finds certain apparent Laws of Life in operation in the Universe to which all Life, in all of its aspects, is apparently amenable. And he feels justified in considering these Laws constant, and invariable, and unchangeable so long as the Universe, as it now is, exists.

And with the above views in mind, this book will proceed to a consideration of its subject, without attempting to peer behind the veil separating the Universe from its Causer—Life from its Source.

But in justice to reader, subject and writer, the latter has thought it well to state that he *does* recognize, not only the veil, but That-which-is-behind-the-Veil. To proceed without this statement would be unfair and misleading. The writer wishes to be understood positively upon this point, even though the declaration may bring forth the derisive jeer of those who feel that they "have outgrown" this conception; or else the calm, superior, pitying smile of those who feel that the Universe is its own Cause and Effect. By "Universe," the writer means "The whole body of Things" (Webster). His declaration means that he believes in "That-which-is-above-Things."

The writer prefers not to attempt to "define" THAT which he calls "The Infinite." The word "Infinite" means "without limit in time, space, power, capacity, knowledge or excellence" (Webster). And to "define" is to "limit"; "mark the limits of"; "mark the end of," etc. The term "define," as applied to "The Infinite," is ridiculous—an absurd paradox. The writer echoes Spinoza's statement: "To define God is to deny Him." And so there shall be no attempt at definition or limitation.

But the human mind, in considering the subject, is bound by its own laws to think of "The Infinite" as Real, and actually being and existent, if it thinks of It at all. And if it thinks of It as "Infinite," it *must*, by its own laws, think of It as Causeless; Eternal; Absolute; Everywhere-present; All-Powerful; All-Wise. The human mind is *compelled* to so consider The Infinite, if it thinks of It at all. But even in so thinking of It as "being" these things, it is doing something like "defining" or "limiting" It, for The Infinite must not only "be" those things, but it must "be" so much more, that "those things" are but as a grain of dust on the desert as compared to the real "Being" of The Infinite. For the "things" mentioned are but "finite" or "defined" things—things possessed by the Finite Things—and, at the best can be but symbols of the attributes or qualities of The Infinite; even the words "attributes" or "qualities" being an absurdity as applied to The Infinite. This view, also, *must* be reported by the human reason, if it thinks about the matter at all.

The final report of the human reason regarding this matter is that it is insoluble and unthinkable to that reason, in its final analysis. This because the human reason is compelled to use terms, concepts, etc., derived from its experience with finite things, and therefore has no tools, measurements, or other appliances with which to "think" of The Infinite. All that it can do is to report that it finds that it has limits itself, and that it finds beyond those limits That which it cannot define, but which it is justified in considering as Infinite, and superior to all finite conceptions, such as Time, Space, Causation and Thought. (The idea of Thought being finite, equally with Time, Space and Causation, is not common, by the writer is compelled to place it in that category, because it is clearly under the laws of Time, Space, and Cause and Effect, and must be considered as "finite." The "knowledge" possessed by The Infinite must be something far transcending that which we know as the result of "mental operations," or "thinking.")

Certain fundamental truths seem to have been impressed upon the human intellect, and the reason is compelled to report in accordance therewith. But an analysis of these fundamental truths is futile, and the attempt only leads one into wild speculations. The only advantage that comes from the attempt is the strengthening of mental muscle of those who are able to stand the strain of the exercise; and the fact that by such attempt we are made aware that we do not know, and cannot know, by reasons of the nature of the Intellect, and are thus prevented from harboring absurd and childish theories about the Unknowable. To know that we do *not* know, and *cannot* know, is the next best thing to actually knowing.

The writer does not wish to be understood, that the limits of the human reason are unalterably fixed. On the contrary, he believes that additional fundamental portions of Truth are super-imposed upon the mind of the race from time to time. And he believes, yes, *knows*, that there are regions of the mind that give reports higher than those conveyed through the Intellect. And he believes that there are phases of knowledge in store for Man that will raise him as much higher than his present position, as that present position is superior to that of the earthworm. And he believes that there are Beings in existence to-day, on planes of Life as yet undreamed of by the average man, who far transcend Man in power, wisdom and nature. He believes that Man is merely just entering into his kingdom, and does not realize the grandeur of that which is his Divine Inheritance.

It will be as well to mention here that the classification of Mind with the aspects of Life, in conjunction with Substance, and Motion, does not mean that the Ego or Man is a material thing. The writer believes that the Ego is a transcendent Being, partaking in some wonderful way of the essence of The Infinite—that it is a Soul—Immortal. He believes that as Paul says, "We are all children of God, but what we shall be does not as yet appear." These matters shall not be discussed in this book, but the writer wishes to make himself clear, in order to prevent misunderstanding. Again, in this respect, he must "fly in the face of Materialism."

But, although the writer expresses his belief in the existence of The Infinite, and bases his philosophy upon that basis, he does not wish to insist upon the identification of his conception with that of any other particular conception of the Source of Life. Nor does he insist upon names, or terms, in connection with the conception. He has used the term, "The Infinite," because it seems to be broader than any other of which he could think, but he uses it merely as a name for the Un-Nameable. So, if the reader prefers, he, or she, may use the terms: "God"; "Deity"; "First Cause"; "Principle"; "Unknowable"; "Infinite and Eternal Energy"; "The Thing-in-Itself"; "The Absolute"; or any of the other countless terms used by Man in his attempt to name the Un-Nameable—to describe the Un-Describable—to define the Un-Definable.

And all may retain their ideas, or lack of ideas, regarding the relation of The Infinite to their own particular religious views, or lack of views. The philosophy of this book need not disturb a man's religious belief—nor does it insist upon the man holding any special religious belief. Those are matters entirely for the exercise of the man's own reason and conscience. And they may retain their own pet philosophy regarding the origin, purposes or plan of the production and existence of the Universe—this book shall not meddle with their metaphysics or philosophy. What is herein offered may be assimilated with the fundamental ideas of nearly every form of religious or philosophical belief, it being in the nature of an Addition rather than a Subtraction, or Division. Its philosophy is Constructive rather than Destructive.

CHAPTER-II

Things As They Are

IN our last chapter we considered the Source-of-All-Things, which we called The Infinite. In this chapter we shall consider the All-Things itself, which men call The Universe. Note that the word Universe is derived from the Latin word "Unus," meaning "One," and "*Versor*," meaning "to turn," the combined word meaning, literally, "One that turns, or moves." The Latin words indicate a close meaning, namely, One thing in motion, turning its several aspects, and assuming many changes of appearance.

The writer does not intend touching upon theories of the origin of the Universe, nor of its purpose, or of any design in its production or management, nor of its possible or probable end. These questions do not belong to our subject, and then again, as was said in the last chapter, speculation regarding it is devoid of results, and leads one to quicksands and bogs of mental reasoning, from which it is difficult to extract oneself. The answer to the Riddle of the Universe rests with The Infinite.

But it is different with the case of the manifested Universe that is evidenced by our senses. Science is a different thing from metaphysics, and its process and mode of work are along different lines. And, much knowledge of Things may be obtained from a consideration of it—remembering always, that its knowledge is confined to Things, and not to That-which-is-back-of-Things. And, so let us consider the Universe of Things.

Material Science has held that the Universe is composed of two principles, (1) Matter; (2) Energy or Force. Some hold that these two principles really are aspects of the same thing, and that there is really but one Principle, one aspect of which is shape, form, etc., and called Matter; the other a quality manifesting in Motion, which quality is called Force. Others, the most radical, hold that there is nothing but Matter, and that Force and Energy is but a "quality," or "power," inherent in Matter. Others hold that Force is the "real thing" and Matter but a form of Force. All branches hold to the idea that Matter and Energy are always found together, and can not be thought of separately. Matter and Force are held to be Eternal, and Infinite, it following that there can be no addition to, or subtraction from either; all apparent loss and gain, creation and destruction being but change of form or mode. God is declared unnecessary, and the Universe is held to operate according to certain Laws of Matter or Force (either or both) which are unchangeable and immutable—eternal and always valid. Mind and Thought are held to be products of properties of Matter or Force (one or both), secreted, evolved, or produced in the Brain. The Soul is relegated to the waste heap, and discarded as useless in the new philosophy. *Moleschott* said, "Thought is a motion of Matter"; and *Holbach*, that "Matter enjoys the power of thinking." "Natural Laws" are held to be sufficient for the explanation of all phenomena, although ignoring the fact that the reason has never before formed the conception of a "law," without thinking it necessary to think of a "law-maker," or a power to enforce and administer the law. However, the philosophers hold that it is no more difficult to think of such a law than to try to form an idea of Space or Eternity, both of which are unthinkable to the human reason, but both of which are admitted as self-evident facts.

But notwithstanding this somewhat crude and "raw" reasoning, Material Science has accomplished a wonderful work in the world, and has brought to light facts of inestimable value to Man in mastering the material world, and in forming correct ideas of the solution of material difficulties. The facts of Material Science enables the world to cheerfully overlook its theories. And even the theories are rapidly undergoing a change, and, as we have stated, some of the most advanced scientists are rapidly reaching the position of the Occultists and mystics, bringing with them a mass of facts to back them up, to exhibit to the Occultists who dealt with principles rather than with details, or material facts, so far as fundamental theories were concerned. Each is boring his way through the mountain tunnel of the Unknown, and both will meet in the centre, their lines meeting each other without a variation. But the Occultists will call the tunnel-centre Mind, and the scientists will call it Matter, but both will be speaking of the same thing. And the Causer of the mountain will probably know that they both are right.

But, we are speaking of the new school of advanced Material Science now—not of the old conservative "All is Matter" people, who have been left behind. The new school speaks of Substance now, instead of Matter, and ascribes to "Substance" the properties of Matter, Energy, and something that they call Sensation, by which they mean Mind in a crude form, and from which they say Mind and "Soul" evolved.

This new school of Scientists are very different from their predecessors—they are less "hide-bound," and far from being so "cock-sure." They are seeing Matter melting into Energy, and giving signs of Sensation, and they are beginning to feel that, after all, there must be a Thing-in-Itself, that is the real basis of, or "real thing" in Substance. There is heard very little among them about "dead matter"; "blind force"; or of the "mechanical theory" of Life and the Universe. Instead of it being a big machine, operated under mechanical laws, with Life as the steam, the Universe is beginning to be regarded as somehow filled with Life, and Science is finding new examples of Life in unexpected quarters, and the "dead matter" area is being narrowed.

Men who have followed the advances made by recent Science are holding their breaths in awe and earnest expectation—and those who are pushing the inquiries and investigations to the furthest extent are showing by their eager faces and trembling hands that they feel that they are very close to the border line separating the old Materialism from a New Science that will give Thought and Philosophy a new impetus and a new platform. Such men are feeling that they are seeing the old Matter melting away into something else—the old theories are falling apart under the light of new discoveries—and these men feel that they are penetrating a new and hitherto unexplored region of the Unknown. May success be theirs, for they are now on the right road to Truth.

In the following chapters we shall see frequent references to "Science"—and when we use the word we shall know it means this new school of Scientists, rather than the older school that is now being superceded. There is no conflict between True Occultism and True Science, notwithstanding their directly opposite theories and ideals—they are merely looking at the Truth from different viewpoints—at different sides of the same shield. A better day is coming, when they shall work together, instead of in opposition. There should be no partisanship in the search for Truth.

Things have worked this way: Occultism would enunciate a theory or principle—but would not attempt to prove it by material facts, for it had not gathered the facts, having found the principle *within* the mind, rather than without. Then, after laughing at the occult theory or principle, Science would search diligently for material facts to prove an opposite theory, and in so doing would unearth new facts that would support the Occultists contention. Then Science would discard its old theory (that is, the younger men would—the old ones, never) and proceed to proclaim a new theory or principle, under a new name, and backed up with a mass of facts and experiments that would create a new school with many enthusiastic followers. The old claim of the Occultists would then be forgotten or else go unrecognized under its old name; or disguised by the fantastic and *bizarre* coverings which some so-called Occultists had draped around the original Truth.

But, so long as Truth is being uncovered, what matters it who does the work, or by what name he calls his school. The movement is ever forward, and upward—what matter the banner under which the armies move?

In this book the writer will advance a very different theory of the Universe of All-Things from that of Modern Science, although he feels that his theory may easily be reconciled with the most advanced views of that school.

In the first place, as he has stated in the first chapter, he does not hold that the Universe, as we know it, is self-sufficient, but he recognizes a Something back of all phenomena and appearances, which Something he calls "The Infinite."

And he differs very materially from the views of those who claim that Mind is but a property, or quality, or something proceeding from Matter or Force, or Matter-Force, or Force-Matter—according to the views of the respective schools. He takes an entirely different and opposite position.

He holds that all that we call Matter (or Substance) and Mind (*as we know it*) are but aspects of something infinitely higher, and which may be called the "Cosmic Mind." He holds that *what we call* "Mind" is but a partial manifestation of the Cosmic Mind. And that Substance or Matter is but a cruder or grosser form of that which we call Mind, and which has been manifested in order to give Mind a Body through which to operate. But this view he merely states in passing, for he makes no attempt to demonstrate or prove the same, his idea being that it forms a different part of the general subject than the phase of "Dynamic Thought," to the consideration of which this book is devoted.

He also differs very materially from the Materialistic school in his conception of Force or Energy. Instead of regarding Force as a distinct principle, and as something of which Mind is but a form, he walks boldly out into the arena of Scientific Thought, and throwing down his gauntlet, proclaims his theory that "There is no such thing as Force apart from Life and Mind"—"All Force and Energy is the product of Life and Mind—all Force, Energy and Motion result from Vital-Mental Action—all Force,

Energy and Motion is Vital-Mental Force, Energy and Motion."—"The Mind abiding in and permeating all Substance, not only has the power to Think, but also the power to Act, and to manifest Force and Energy, which are its inherent and essential properties."

He also takes the position that Mind is in and about and around Everything. And that "Everything is Alive and Thinking." And that there is no such things as "Dead-Matter," or "Blind-Force," but that all Substance, even to the tiniest Particle, is permeated with Life and Mind, and that all Force and Motion is caused and manifested by Mind.

He holds that all forms of Force, Energy and Motion, from the Attraction of the Particles of Matter, and their movements in response thereto, up to the Attraction of Gravitation, and the response of the Worlds, and Suns, and Stars, and Planets, thereto—are forms of Mental Energy and Force, and Action. And that from the tiniest atom, or particle, to the greatest Sun—all obey this Great Action of Mind—this Great Force of Mind—this Great Energy of Mind—this Great Power of Mind.

And upon this rock—this rock of Truth, he believes it to be—he takes his stand, and announces his belief, and bids all-comers take notice of what he believes to be a germ-thought that will grow, develop, and increase so that it will eventually permeate all Scientific Thought as the years roll along. He calls this theory "The Theory of Dynamic Thought."

CHAPTER-III

The Universality of Life And Mind

THE writer has deemed it advisable to preface his consideration of "Mind" in itself, as well as of Substance and Motion, with two chapters, the purpose of which will be to demonstrate that Mind, in some form or degree, is to be found in connection with all Things—and that Everything has Life—and that Mind is an accompaniment of all Life. To many the term "Mind" means only the "thinking quality" of man, or perhaps of the lower animals; and "Life" the property only of such organic creatures. For that reason it has been deemed advisable to point out that Life and Mind are found even in the lowest forms of substance—even in the inorganic world.

In this chapter and from now on, the writer shall use the term "*the* Mind," etc., to indicate the particular mental principle of the creature or thing—the bit of Mind that is segregated from the rest, and which each person thinks of as "mine," just as he thinks of "my" body, as distinguished from the universal supply of Substance. The term "Mind" will be used in its Universal sense.

And, the writer intends to use Elmer Gates' term, "*Mentation*," in the sense of "effort; action; or effect; in or of, the Mind"—in short, "mental process." The word is useful and when one has learned to use it, he will prefer it to the more complicated terms. Remember, then, please—"Mentation" means "Mental Process." Mentation includes that which we call "Thought," as well as some more elementary forms of mental process that we are not in the habit of dignifying by the term, Thought, which latter we usually reserve for mental process of a higher order.

So, then, "Mind" is the something of which one's particular Mind is composed; "The Mind" is that something possessed by one, by and through which he "thinks"; "Mentation" is mental process; and "Thought" is a advanced kind of Mentation. At least, the said words will be so employed in this book, from now on.

In this chapter, you are asked to consider the fact that Life is Universal—that Everything is Alive. And, that Mind and Mentation is an attribute of Life, and that, consequently, Everything has Mind, and is able to express a degree of Mentation.

Forms of Life, as we know them, are always seen as possessing two aspects, *viz.*, (1) Body (Substance); and (2) Mentation (Mind). The two aspects are always found in combination. There may be living creatures who occupy bodies of so fine a form of Substance as to be invisible to the human senses—but their bodies would be "Substance" just as much as is the "body" of the granite rock. And, in order to "think," these beings would need to have a material something corresponding to the brain, though it be finer in quality than the rarest gas, vapor, of electric wave. No body, without Mentation; no Mentation without a body. This last is the invariable law of the world of Things. And naught but The Infinite—That-which-is-above-Things—can be exempt from that law.

In order to grasp the idea of the Universality of Mind, let us go back to the elementary forms of Things, and, step by step, see how Mentation manifests itself in every point on the scale from mineral to man—using bodies ranging from the hardest rock to that finest form of known Substance—the Brain of Man. As Mind advances in the scale of evolution it creates its own working instrument—the body (including the brain) and shapes, and moulds it to admit of the fullest possible expression of Mentation possible at that stage. Mind is the moulder—body (and brain) that which is moulded. And Inclination, Desire, and Will, are the motive powers leading to gradual Unfoldment, the impelling cause being the craving for Satisfaction.

We shall make our journey backward—and ignoring Beings higher in the scale, we shall start with Man. Leaving out of the consideration, for the moment, the fact of the existence of the "Ego," or "Spirit" of Man, which is higher than Body or Mind—and considering "the Mind of Man," rather than the Man himself—we have our starting point on the downward journey of investigation. We need not devote much attention to the consideration of the Mind of Man, at this stage, although we shall have much to do with it, later on.

But we may undertake a brief consideration of the descending degrees of Mentation as manifested by Man, as we pass down the scale in the human family, considering in turn, the Newtons, Shakespeares, Emersons, Edisons, and their brothers in intellect, in the field of mathematics, literature, music, art, invention, science, statesmanship, business, skilled workmanship, etc., respectively. From these high levels we pass down, gradually, through the strata of men of but a slightly lower degree of intellect—down through the strata of the "average man"—down through the strata of the ignorant man—down through the strata of the lowest type of our own race and time—down through the strata of the barbarian, then on to the savage, then on to the Digger Indian, the Bushman. What a difference from highest to lowest—a being from another world would doubt that they were all of the same family.

Then we pass rapidly through the various strata of the lower animal kingdom—from the comparatively high degree of Mentation of the horse, the dog, the elephant, etc., down through the descending scale of the mammals, the degree of Mentation becoming less marked at each step of the journey. Then on through the bird kingdom. Then through the world of reptiles. Then through the family of fishes. Then through the millions of forms of insect life, including those wonderful creatures, the ant and the bee. Then on through the shell-fish family. Then on through the community of sponges, polyps, and other low forms of life. Then on to the vast empire of the microscopic creatures, whose name is legion. Then on to the plant life, the highest of which have "sensitive cells" that resemble brains and nerves—descending by stages to the lower plant life. Then still lower to the world of bacteria, microbes, and infusoria—the groups of cells with a common life—the monera—the single cell. The mind that has followed us in this descent of life, from the highest form to the cell-like "thing" merely "existing" in the slime at the bottom of the ocean, has acquired a sense of awe and sublimity not dreamed of by "the man on the street."

The degrees of Mentation in the lower animal kingdom are well known to all of us, therefore, we need not devote much time to their consideration at this time. Although the degree of Mentation in some of the lowly forms of animal life, are scarcely above that of the plant life (in fact, are inferior to that of the highest plants), still we have accustomed ourselves to the use of the word "Mind" in connection with even the lowest animals, while we hesitate to apply the word to the plants.

It is true that some of us do not like to think of the lower animals "reasoning," so we use the word "Instinct" to denote the degree of Mentation of the lower animal. The writer does not object to the word; in fact, he shall use it for the sake of distinguishing between the several mental states. But, remember, "Instinct" is but a term used to denote a lesser form of "Reason"—and the "Instinct" of the horse or dog is a fine thing when we consider the "Reason" of the Bushman or Digger Indian. However, we shall not quarrel about words. Both "Reason" and "Instinct" mean degrees or forms of "Mentation," the word we are using. The lower forms of animal life exhibit Mentation along the lines of sex-action; feeling and taste. Then by degrees come smell, hearing and sight. And then something very like "reasoning" in the case of the dog, elephant, horse, etc. Mentation everywhere in the animal kingdom, in some degree. No doubt about Life and Mentation, there.

But what about Mentation and Life in the plant life? All of you admit that there is "Life" there—but about Mentation, well, let us see! Some of you draw the line at the word "Mind" in connection with plants, although you freely admit the existence of "Life" there. Well, remember our axiom—"no Life without Mentation." Let us try to apply it.

A moment's reflection will give you instances of Mentation among the plants. Science has called it "Appetency," rather than admit "Mind," the word "Appetency" being defined as "an instinctive tendency on the part of low forms of organic life to perform certain acts necessary for their well-being—such as to select and absorb such particles of matter as serve to support and nourish them." Well, that looks like a degree of Mentation, doesn't it? Many young animals evidence little or nothing more than "Appetency" in suckling. We shall adopt the word "Appetency" to designate the Mentation in plant-life. Remember this, please.

Anyone who has raised trees or plants has noticed the instinctive efforts of the plant to reach the water and sunlight. Potatoes in dark cellars have been known to send forth shoots twenty feet in length in order to reach an opening in the wall. Plants have been known to bend over during the night and dip their leaves in a pot of water several inches away. The tendrils of climbing plants seek for the stake or support, and find it, too, although it has been changed daily. The tendril will retwine itself, after it has been untwisted and bent in another direction. The tips of the roots of the tree are said to show a sensitiveness almost akin to that of the limb of an animal, and evidently possess something akin to nerve matter.

Duhamel placed some beans in a cylinder of moist earth. When they began to sprout, he turned the cylinder around quarter way of its circumference; then a little more the next day; and so on, a little each day, until the cylinder had described a complete revolution—had been turned completely around. Then the beans were taken from the earth, and lo! the roots and sprouts formed a complete spiral. With every turn of the cylinder the roots and sprouts had changed their position and direction—the roots striving to grow "downward," and the sprouts striving to grow "upward"—until the spiral had formed. Akin to this is the boy's trick of uprooting a sprouting seed, and replanting it upside down, in which case the sprouts begin to turn a semicircle until it is able to grow straight up to the surface of the earth, while the roots describe a semicircle until they can grow downward once more.

And so on, story after story of "Appetency" or Mentation in plants might be told, until we reach the insect-catching species, when even the most conservative observer is forced to admit that: "Well, it does *almost* seem like thinking, doesn't it?" Any lover of plants, flowers or trees, and who has been able to study them at first hand, does not need much argument to prove that plant-life exhibits traces of Mentation, some of it pretty far advanced, too. Some lovers of plants go so far as to claim that one must "love" plants before they will succeed in growing them, and that the plants feel and respond to the feeling. But the writer does not insist upon this, but merely mentions it in passing.

Before leaving the subject of Mentation in plants, the writer is tempted to steal a little more space and tell you that plants do more than receive sensations of light and moisture. They exhibit rudimentary taste as well. Haeckel relates an interesting story of an insect-catching plant. He states that while it will bend its leaves when any solid body (excepting a raindrop) touches its surface, still it will secrete its acrid digestive fluid only when that object happens to be nitrogenous (meat or cheese). The plant is able to distinguish its meat diet (its food being insectivorous), and while it will supply its gastric juice for meat and cheese, as well as for the insect, it will not do so for other solids to which it is indifferent. He also mentions the fact that roots of trees and plants are able to taste the different qualities of soil, and will avoid poor soil and plunge into the richer parts of the earth. The sexual organism and life of plants also affords a great field for study to the student hunting for evidences of "life" and "Mentation" in that kingdom.

The motion or circulation of the sap in trees and plants was formerly considered to be due to capillary attraction and purely "mechanical laws," but recent scientific experiments have shown it to be a vital action—an evidence of life and Mentation—the experiments having proven that if the cell-substance of the plant was poisoned or paralyzed, the circulation of sap immediately ceased, although the "mechanical principles" had not been interfered with in the least.

And now on to the mineral kingdom. "What," you may cry, "Mind and Mentation in the mineral and chemical world—surely not?" Yes, even in these low planes may be found traces of mental action. There is Life everywhere—even there. And where there is Life there is Mind. Away back among the chemical principles, and the minerals we may go in our search for Life and Mind—they cannot escape us—even there!

CHAPTER-IV

Life And Mind Among The Atoms

TO the majority of persons the title of this chapter would seem an absurdity. Not to speak of Inorganic "Mind," the idea of "Life" in the Inorganic World would seem a ridiculous paradox to the "man on the street" who thinks of Substance as "dead," lifeless and inert. And, to tell the truth, even Science has held this view until a comparatively recent period, laughing to scorn the old Occult Teaching that the Universe is Alive, and capable of Thinking. But the recent discoveries of modern Science has changed all this, and we no longer hear Science speaking of "dead Matter" or "blind Force"—it recognizes that these terms are meaningless, and that the dreams of the old Occultists are coming true. Science confronts a live and thinking Universe. She is dazzled by the sight, and would shade her eyes, fearing to see that which she feels must present itself to her vision when her eyes become accustomed to the sight.

But a few daring minds among the scientific investigators are dreaming wonderful dreams to-day, and they tell us in broken tones of the wonderful visions that are passing before their sight. They dare not tell it all, for they fear the ridicule of their fellows. Their visions are of Life—Universal Life. In its investigations of the Material, Science has penetrated so far into the recesses of Things that its most advanced thinkers and investigators now find themselves standing in the presence of the Immaterial.

Science to-day is proclaiming the new doctrine—that is the same as the "old" doctrine of the Occultists—the doctrine of "Life Everywhere"—Life even in the hardest rock!

Before entering into our consideration of the evidence of Mentation in the Inorganic world, let us accustom ourselves to the idea of "something like Life" being found there. It will be better for us to approach the subject by easy stages. Where there is Life there must be Mind—so let us first look for evidences of Life.

The "man on the street" would require something more tangible than scientific explanations of "sensation," "attraction," etc. What can we offer him as an illustration? Let us see!

Suppose we call the attention of "the man" to the fact that metals get tired after considerable work without periods of rest. Science calls this the "fatigue of elasticity." When the metals are given rest, they recuperate and regain their former elasticity and health. "The man" may remember that his razor acts this way occasionally—and if he talks the matter over with his barber, his suspicions will be verified.

Then, if he consults a musician friend, he will be informed that tuning-forks also become tired, and lose their vibrating quality, until they are given a rest. Then his machinist friend will tell him that machinery in factories must be given a rest, occasionally, else it will begin to disintegrate and "die." Machinery will go on a strike for a rest, if it is overworked.

Then metals contract disease. Science informs us that zinc and tin have been infected, and the infection has spread from sheet to sheet crumbling the metal into powder—the spread of the infection resembling the spread of a plague among animals or plant-life. Science has experimented with copper and iron, and has found that these metals may be poisoned with chemicals, and will remain in a weakened condition until antidotes are administered. Window-glass workers declare that there is such a thing as "glass-disease," that will ruin fine stained glass windows unless the infected panes are removed. The "glass-disease" starts with one pane, and spreads gradually to the entire window, and from there to other windows.

Metallurgists have found that when metallic ores are put under certain forms of pressure, they seem to lose strength, and become weak until the pressure is removed.

Do these things mean anything to the "Man of the Street?"

Another step in the consideration of Life in the Inorganic world, is the realization of the fact that, after all, there is but the very finest line separating the higher forms of Mineral "life," from the lower forms of vegetable life, or the life of those "Things" which we may call either plants or animals. The "Life-line" is being pushed further back every day, by scientific investigation, and the "living" thing of today was the "inanimate" thing of yesterday. We hear much talk in the newspapers about some scientist, or another, "discovering life," or "creating life," in some "inanimate substance." Bless your hearts, you who are alarmed by these reports—no one can "create" life in anything, for it already exists there. The "discovery" is simply the realization of this fact.

Science, by means of the microscope, has brought to light forms of "living things," resembling in appearance the fine dust of inorganic minerals. These low forms of life exhibit but the simplest vital processes, the same very closely resembling chemical processes, although just a shade higher in the scale. Living creatures have been found which could be dried and laid aside like dust for several years, and then revived by being immersed in water, when they would resume their vital process as if they had been awakened from a sleep. Forms of life, called "Baccilli" have been discovered that can pass through degrees of heat and cold that can be expressed only by vague symbols or figures, the heat and cold being so intense that the unscientific mind cannot imagine it.

In appearance the "Diatoms" resemble the chemical crystals. These "Diatoms" are minute one-celled living "Things," having a hard but thin siliceous covering or shell, of extreme delicacy. They are what are known as "microscopic" creatures—that is, visible only through the microscope. Some of them are so small that it would take a thousand or more to cover the head of a pin. But, remember this—the microscope reveals them as "living creatures" performing vital functions. They are found in the deep waters of the ocean. To the naked eye they appear like fine sand or "dirt," but under the most powerful microscope, they are seen to comprise many species and varieties, exhibiting many peculiar shapes and forms—in fact, they have been called "living geometrical forms," their shapes and appearances almost exactly resembling those of the chemical and mineral crystals.

Science informs us that these and similar microscopic creatures, number thousands of families or species,—and it is thought that the varieties of microscopic creatures outnumber the varieties of creatures visible to the unaided sight. And, remember, that there is probably a still greater world of "sub-microscopic" creatures, that is a world invisible even when the most powerful microscope is used. Who knows what wonders are to be found there—what forms of creatures live, and move and have their being there.

In passing by the subject of the resemblance between the outward forms of living things and the crystals, it is interesting to note how the crystals of frost and ice resemble the forms of leaves, branches, flowers, foliage, etc.—the pane of glass covered with these frosty forms, resembles a garden. The disk of saltpeter, under the effect of polarized light, very closely resembles the form of the orchid.

Recent scientific experiments have shown that certain metallic salts, when subjected to a galvanic current, group themselves around one of the poles of the battery, and assume a mushroom-like shape and appearance. At first, they seem to be transparent, but gradually they assume color, the top becoming a bright red, with the under-side showing a pale rose color, the stem being of a pale straw color. The discoverers of these peculiar forms, called them by the German equivalent for "inorganic mushrooms," but even this term seems scarcely worthy of them, for they even show a trace of something like organs. Under the microscope they are seen to have fine canals or vein-like channels running through their stems, from top to base. And through these "veins" the "thing" absorbed fresh material and actually "grew" like low forms of fungus-life. Were these things merely minerals or chemical-substances, or were they low forms of organic life? The lines between the Inorganic and the Organic are being wiped out rapidly. The Supreme Power that *caused* Life to Be, caused it to All, and did not divide Its manifestations into Dead-Things and Live-Things, but breathed into all the Breath of Life. And the more clearly we see the actual evidence of this, the greater does that Supreme Power seem to us.

A very low form of living creatures called the Monera, is held by Science to be the one of the strands of the connecting link between the organic and inorganic worlds. The Monera are the lowest and simplest form (at least so far known) of organic life. They may be said to be "organic" creatures *without organs*—being but little more than simple cells—tiny globules of plasm, surrounded by a thin membrane—their sole vital function being the absorption of nourishment through the pores of their covering (just as a piece of chalk would absorb water) and the consequent conversion of the nourishment into material for growth, the whole process resembling chemical action. The Monera reproduce their kind simply by cleavage or separation of the substance of the mother cell into two, and so on, being little more than the "growth" of crystals. The Monera are everywhere recognized, without question, as "living creatures," but they exhibit merely a trace more of life than do certain forms of crystals.

The difficulty in considering crystals as "living things" is partially due to the outward form and substance, so different from the form and substance of the higher "living things." But we have seen that the Diatoms took on shapes of crystals, and that the outer shell or covering was similar to silicia, a mineral, the inner substance being but a tiny speck of plasm, similar to that of the substance of a plant cell. And then we may look to the tiny bit of chalk dust which was once the skeleton-form of a living creature. The same is true of coral. In the very low forms of life, the skeleton, or form, is the thing most apparent, the plasm of "living substance" being still smaller, and less apparent. And yet, the skeleton, or shell, was formed by the vital processes of the creature, and was a part of its "body," just as is the skeleton or bony structure of the higher animals. And, in the same sense it is "living substance." And, remember, that there is but little difference between these "bodies" of the low forms of life, and the bodies of crystals. And the chemical constituents of its plasmic inner body is but slightly different from that of the crystals. And its nature and vital process are by a shade higher in the scale than those of the crystals.

You may ask why we have said so much of Crystals. The reason is just this—Science has begun to think of Crystals as semi-living things, and its most advanced investigators and thinkers go further and assert that "the Crystals are alive—Crystallization is an evidence of life process."

Crystals arrange themselves in well-known and well-defined shapes, direction and order of formation being observed implicitly. Each crystal follows the laws and habits of its kind, just as do plants and animals. Its lines of crystallization are mathematically perfect, and according to the laws of its being. Not only this, but some substances have a range of six or seven different forms of crystal-forms possible to them. In some cases a chemical element assumes one form of crystallization when it manifests as one mineral, and a second form when it manifests in another form—in each case however, it manifests along well-known and recognized courses of action, movement, and shapes.

Crystals may be "killed" by a strong electrical discharge—that is, they are so affected that they disintegrate, their atoms separating to form new combinations, just as is the case with the "bodies" of higher forms of life. Some scientists have gone so far as to claim that they had discovered something akin to rudimentary sex-action in certain crystals, resembling the sex-process of the lowest plant-life. But this has not, as yet, been positively established, although it seems probable and reasonable. A recent writer in one of the magazines has said, "Crystallization, as we are to learn now, is not a mere mechanical grouping of dead atoms. It is a birth." This may seem mere "scientific poetry" until the process of crystallization is carefully studied, when it will be seen to give evidence, not only of something like vital and mental action, but also something very much like reproductive functioning of the lower forms of "life."

There is an "assimilation" of material to build up the crystal in the first place, just as an animal assimilates matter to build up its shell—or a tree to form its bark. The "form" of the crystal is truly its "body," and behind and *in that body there is "something at work" that is not the body, but which is forming it*. And, later on, that crystal increases in size, and then begins to separate into two, throwing off a smaller crystal, identical in form with the parent crystal. This manner of reproduction is almost identical with the process of reproduction in the lower forms of "life," which consist merely of a like separation of the parent form into two, and the throwing off of the offspring.

The principal difference between the growth of crystals and of the Monera, is that the Crystals grow by absorbing fresh matter and attaching it to their outer surface, while the Monera grow by absorbing fresh material and growing outwardly, from within. But this may be accounted for by the difference in the density of their bodies, the Crystal being very solid, while the Monera is like a thin jelly. If the Crystal had a soft interior, it could grow like the Monera or Diatom, *but then it would be a Diatom*.

The process of crystallization is accountable only by the theory that in the crystal there exists something like life and Mentation. There is something more than mere "mechanical motion," or blind chance at work here. Does not the process of crystallization look like rudimentary purposive action? It may be said that it is movement and action in accordance with some established "Law of Nature"—granted, but is not that also true of the physical processes and growth of higher forms of life? Is the forming of the Crystal-form to be considered as a "mechanical effect," and the forming of the "shell" of the Monera to be considered a "mental and vital action?" If so, wherefore?

The point is that Crystals act as if they are "alive," and capable of assimilation, growth, and reproduction, in a manner and degree differing but very slightly from corresponding functioning of the lower forms of "life." Verily the Crystals are "alive"—and if alive they must have at least a trace of "Mind." Does it not appear that they exhibit something very like both? Quoting from a recent writer, let us notice that: "Recent investigations in the new department of science, which has been termed 'plasmology,' show in crystals phenomena which are absolutely analogous to vital phenomena—so much so that photographs of certain forms produced in the changes of crystals appear to be almost exact duplicates of those in the various lower forms of microbes. The question has been raised as to whether the microbe is no more alive than the crystal, or the latter equally endowed with life as is the former."

And now another step, in our search for Life. Remember, that the hardest rocks are composed of crystals of certain kinds. And, if the higher crystals have Life, then it is only fair to suppose that the lower and cruder forms are likewise endowed, even if in a still lower degree. And if all crystals are endowed with Life, then the most solid rocks, being composed of aggregations of crystals must be masses of Inorganic Life—and consequently, of Inorganic Mind. A Crystal, according to Webster, is "the regular form, bounded by plane surfaces, which a substance tends to assume in solidifying, through the inherent powers of cohesive attraction."

That definition of Webster tells the whole story, and we see that a "Crystal" is merely a "regular form" of a "Substance," which the substance "tends to assume in solidifying"—that is in re-assuming a solid form after being in a liquid or melted state, and that is just what all the rocks of the earth did when they emerged from the melted state in which they existed in the early days of the world's history. And this "tendency" that caused them to solidify, and assume certain crystal forms, and which must have existed potentially through the melted state—what of that, what is this "tendency" or force. The definition answers: "*the inherent powers of cohesive attraction.*"

So, here is "Cohesive Attraction," that we shall consider fully in forthcoming chapters of this book. "Inherent," too, the definition says. What is "Inherent?" Let us see, Webster defines "Inherent" as "permanently existing." So this power of Cohesive Attraction "permanently existed" in the Substance or else in connection with it. Let us take another look at Cohesive Attraction.

Cohesive Attraction is that form of Universal Attraction that causes the Molecules of a body to draw together—that "invisible power of" the Molecule, by which it draws another Molecule toward itself, and itself toward the other, the manifestation of which power by several Molecules tends to draw each of them together. (We shall learn of these particles of Substance called Molecules before long.) It is a primal cause of Motion, this mutual Attraction, and drawing-power. Now is it reasonable to suppose that this wonderful "power" is a mere blind-force? Is it not more reasonable to think of it as a form of vital-action—life-action? "Dead" things could not manifest this force and action.

And if this Cohesive Attraction is an evidence of Life, then all substance must have Life manifesting through it. Not only the rocks, but the soil and earth and dirt, for they are but crumbled rock.

And, when we thus consider Substance, as being the "body" through which Life is Manifesting, we must not lose sight of the Molecules and Atoms, in our consideration of the Mass. A bit of rock; crystal; or dirt; is but an aggregation of countless Molecules, grouped together in certain crystallized shapes and forms, each having characteristics of its own. These Molecules cling together, in accordance with their mutual Attractive powers.

And each of these Molecules is composed of a number of Atoms, which cling together in accordance with Chemical Affinity, or Chemism—but which is but another name for Attraction, or Cohesion—and which form a little family, called a Molecule. And these Atoms are composed of Corpuscles. We will waive the consideration of the Corpuscle, for the moment, but even if we consider it, we only carry the subject back a step farther. What we wish to say, could be said even if there were ten further divisions of Substance—or a million, for that matter.

The point we wish you to consider now, is that we must separate the Mass into its constituents—its Molecules, Atoms, and even Corpuscles—in our search for the Life in the Mineral and Chemical World. If there is Life in the Mass, there must be life in the Molecule, Atom, or Corpuscle. Now, do we find it there? Certainly, for the tiniest Atom manifests its Attractive Power, and not only does it draw other atoms to itself by virtue thereof, but it even goes a step further, and shows a "preference"—a degree of "liking" in its mutual relations with other atoms.

We shall see, in future chapters, that there is "desire," "love," "marriage," and "divorce" among the chemical Atoms. We shall consider the flirtations, and love-affairs of certain Atoms. We shall see how an Atom will leave another, and fly to a new charmer. We shall have many evidences of *the Atom's power to receive sensations, and to respond to the same*. Nothing "dead" about this, is there? The Atom is "very much alive." The Attraction; Affinity; and Motions, of the Atom, give a certain evidence of something "very much like Life," as we see it in higher forms. In the Atom exists all the Life that causes crystallization. And in the Atom lies that which causes Force and Motion to manifest. Verily, the Atom lives and moves and has its being.

And, so our journey is ended—we have traced Life to its last stages of manifestations—and we have found it there, and at each step of the journey. But, stop, we have not completed our journey—we have but begun it. "Why," some of us may cry, "how can we go back of the Atom, or Electron?" The answer is "INTO THE ETHER"!

Yes, back of the Atom and the Corpuscle, is said by Science to lie that wonderful, paradoxical Something they call The Universal Ether—that Something that Science has considered the Womb of Matter and Force—Something that is different from Anything ever known or dreamed of by

Man,—that Something which Science has labored so diligently to build up, and which it has used as an "explanation" for so much phenomena, but regarding which, of very recent date, there has begun to grow a distrust and a suspicion, owing to the discovery of Radiant Matter, and things that followed in its train. But, notwithstanding these shadowy suspicions, Science still asserts in belief in the constancy and integrity of The Ether, and it behooves us to investigate that wonderful region in which it dwells, in order to see whether Life and Mind are also to be found there. We think that, in the words of the street, we shall find that they are "very much there."

And, so in later chapters of this book, we shall consider the Etherial Region very fully. But before doing so, we had better give Substance and Motion, in all their forms, a careful consideration, for a correct understanding of them is vitally necessary for an intelligent conception of the ideas underlying the philosophy to be herein set forth.

Now, pray do not leave this chapter with the belief that the writer has said that the Particles of Inorganic Substance are endowed with Conscious reasoning powers. Nothing of the kind has been said—nothing of the kind is meant. The Life and Mind evidenced in the Particles are but the faintest glimmerings. There is no sign of "consciousness" or "reasoning"—the Mind exhibited is less than that of the plant, yes, less than even that of the cell of the plant. The Life is evidenced by power to move, and the Mind is evidenced by the ability to receive impressions and to respond to the same by evidencing Force and movement.

There is no evidence of "consciousness" or "understanding" in these mental processes. Consciousness is not an essential attribute of Life or Mind-action. In fact, but a small part of even the Mentation of Man is performed in the field of consciousness. Nearly all of his bodily functions are beneath the field of consciousness—one does not consciously regulate the beating of his heart; the circulation of his blood; the digestion and assimilation of his food; the tearing-down and building-up work of the cells; the work of the organs, etc., etc. Yes, these processes are all mental processes, and far from mere "mechanical movements," or chemical processes, as some imagine. Let the spark of Life leave the body, and the processes stop, although all the chemicals are still there, and the "mechanical movements" might go on unhindered.

The Particles of Substance have enough Life and Mind to enable them to move, receive and respond to impressions, and to exert force in accordance with the Law of Attraction—but there it stops. The Crystals show signs of something like taking nourishment, but the real taking of food may be said to commence with the Monera. Not until very high degrees of Life and Mind are attained, do "creatures" begin to exhibit Consciousness, and that which is called "Understanding" is still higher in the scale, and not until Man is reached does the faculty of turning the mental searchlight *inward* manifest itself. These matters are mentioned here merely to prevent misunderstanding and misapprehension.

But still, do not forget—the Particles of Substance receive impressions and respond thereto—they *act* and exert Force and Energy—they manifest Life and Mentation.

CHAPTER-V

The Story of Substance

AS we stated in a former chapter, there are two Aspects of All-Things, *viz.*, (1) Substance; (2) Mind. In this and the following two chapters we shall consider the first one, Substance, which Science calls "Matter."

Perhaps it would be as well to begin by asking ourselves the question: "What is Substance?" The answer seems to be: "Anything that takes up room; the Body aspect of Things; matter occupying space, etc." Some writers have spoken of Substance as "something tangible—that can be felt," but this definition will not do, for there are forms of Substance too fine to be felt. And so, perhaps the definition "The Body of Things," is as good a definition as any, taken in connection with the thought that it "takes up room."

Science divides Substance (which it calls "Matter") into four general classes, *viz.*: (1) *Solid Matter*, which is Substance, the parts of which closely adhere and resist impression, such as stone, wood, flesh, etc., the degrees of solidity varying greatly, and sometimes shading into the next class, which is called:

(2) *Liquid Matter*, which may be described as Substance, the parts of which have a free motion among themselves, and easily yield to impression, such as water, molasses, etc., the degree of fluidity ranging from some liquids that flow very slowly, such as hot pitch, up to others that flow very freely, such as water, wine, etc., the property of fluidity being also shared by the next higher class, which is called:

(3) *Aeriform Matter*, which is Substance in the form of "elastic fluid," such as air, gas, vapor, etc.; and

(4) *Radiant Matter*, which is of recent recognition, and which is an ultra-gaseous form of Substance, utterly unlike anything ever before known, consisting of the tiniest particles of "corpuscles" of Substance finer and more subtle than the rarest form of atomic substance known to Science.

The three classes are well represented by (1) Earth (solid); (2) Water (liquid); (3) Air (aeriform); (4) The Corpuscles or Electrons, or particles of electrified substance, first noticed in connection with the X Rays, Radium, etc.

But it must be remembered that these four classes of Substance are not fixed or permanent—on the contrary they are changeable either under pressure, when subjected to heat, or under the influence of electricity, etc. In fact the word "condition" is more applicable than the term "class." The condition or class of a particle of Substance may be changed into another class or condition by the application of the agencies above named. The same substance may exist in two or three classes, under different circumstances. Solids may be changed into liquids, and liquids into gases, and *vice versa*. Metals may be melted, then changed into gas, according to the degree of heat applied. Liquids may be changed into vapor by the application of heat, or into solids by the withdrawal of heat.

For an example we may turn to Water, which is a solid in the condition of ice; a liquid in the condition of water; and steam in the condition of vapor. Quicksilver is a metal which is in a liquid condition in our ordinary temperature, but which becomes a solid when subjected to a very low degree of temperature, and may be transformed into a gas, under a high degree of heat. Air is a vapor in our ordinary temperature, but has been transformed into "liquid air" under tremendous pressure, which produced a very low degree of temperature, and, theoretically, it may be transformed into a solid under a sufficiently low degree of temperature, although so far, Science has not been able to produce a degree of cold sufficient to "freeze" the liquid air. It is all a matter of "freeze," "melt," and "evaporate," in all forms of Substance—and any substance, at least theoretically, is capable of being subjected to any of the three conditions just named, and being manifested in the respective conditions, of Solid, Liquid, and Aeriform.

This may actually be accomplished with the majority of substances at this time, although in some instances we are not able to produce a sufficiently high temperature to "melt and evaporate" certain solid substances, on the one hand, or a sufficiently low degree of temperature to "liquify" or "freeze solid" certain vapors. But the intense heat of the centre of the earth is able to melt rocks, and show them as liquid lava flowing from volcanoes, and Science teaches that the solid Substance of the Earth, and other planets, suns, etc., existed in the shape of a vapor at one time, and would again take on that condition in case of a collision with another great body, which convert motion into intense heat that would first melt, and then vaporize every solid particle of which the earth is composed.

If the sun's heat were completely to die out, the cold would be so intense that the air around the earth, and all the gases and vapors, would be frozen to solids. In physics the term "gas" is generally applied to a substance that is aeriform in our ordinary temperature, but which may be liquefied in a low temperature; the term "vapor" being generally applied to the aeriform condition of substances that are solid or liquid in our ordinary temperatures, but which may be "evaporated" by heat, and thus transformed into an aeriform condition, resuming their original form upon cooling. These terms, however, are technical, and practically there is no difference between a gas and a vapor.

In the above statements regarding the possibility of the transformation of each of the several forms of Substance, into other forms, the reference has been applied only to the three better known forms, *i.e.*, Solid, Liquid and Aeriform. The fourth form or state of Substance, known as Radiant Matter, is of too recent discovery to admit of its properties being accurately observed. The best and latest opinion of Science, however, is that it constitutes what may be called "Primal Matter"—that is substance from which all other forms, states, kinds and varieties of Substance arise—the "stuff" from which they are manufactured. Science seems to be discarding the Ether theory of the Origin of Matter, in favor of this "Primal Matter."

Physical Science divides Substance into Masses, Molecules, and Atoms—that is, the old Physical Science did, but the later investigators now see that even the Atom may be sub-divided. But the old terms may as well be used, at least for the time being. Let us consider these divisions.

A *"Mass"* is a quantity of Substance considered as a whole—but which is composed of a collection or combination of parts (molecules.) A lump of coal; a piece of iron; a portion of meat, even a drop of water, is a Mass. The only requisite for a Mass, is that it contains two or more parts or molecules. Therefore a Mass is a collection or combination of two or more molecules, considered as a whole.

A *"Molecule"* is the *physical* unit of Substance, or, in other words, the smallest part of any kind of Substance that can exist by itself and still remain that particular "kind" of substance. (But not the smallest chemical part—the latter is called an Atom, and Atoms combine to form a Molecule.) The Molecule exists as a unit, and cannot be split or separated by physical means, although it may be separated into Atoms by chemical means. In order that we may form a clear idea of the Molecule, let us take a very small Mass of Matter—a drop of water, for instance. This drop of water is a Mass composed of a great number of molecules. It may be divided, and sub-divided, into smaller and still smaller parts. This division may be carried on until it reaches a point where our sight and instruments are unable to make a further sub-division.

But, theoretically, the work may be carried on still further, until at last a limit is reached where we are unable to divide the water into any smaller parts, without separating its chemical constituents from each other, in which latter case there would be no water at all, its chemical constituents (or Atoms) having separated and now appearing as two atoms of Hydrogen and one atom of Oxygen, separated and apart and no longer forming a molecule of water.

Well, this smallest possible part of water (or any other form of Substance) is a Molecule. Remember the Molecule is the smallest part of that kind of Substance that can be produced by division and sub-division, without destroying the "kind" of the Substance. It is the smallest part of any kind of Substance that can exist by itself, and maintain its "kind."

In order that you may grasp the minuteness of the Molecule, we may mention that Science claims that no molecule, even the largest, is of sufficient magnitude to be seen under even the strongest microscope. It has been calculated that if a drop of water as large as a pea were magnified to the size of the Earth, the molecules would then appear no larger than the original drop. The space between the molecules is believed to be considerably larger than the molecules themselves.

The figures that are necessary to use in connection with molecular Substance are likely to stagger the imagination. Besides speaking of the molecules of inorganic Substance, it may be interesting to note that a spider's thread is so fine that a piece of it large enough to circle the earth would weigh only half a pound. And yet each thread is composed of six thousand filaments. And each of these minute filaments may be divided into tiny bits, and each bit will still be a Mass of Substance containing thousands of molecules and their constituent chemical atoms. There are living, microscopic creatures, so small that five millions of them might be crowded into a space the size of a pin head. And yet each of them have organs. And in these organs fluids circulate. Try to figure out the size of the molecules of the fluids circulating in these tiny organs, not to speak of the chemical atoms.

When you handle a coin, an infinitesimal portion of it is worn off—can you figure the size of the molecules composing that part? When a rose throws off its perfume, it emanates tiny particles of itself—can you measure or weigh the molecules composing that odor? The human mind is compelled to realize its finiteness when it considers these things—but we have only just begun to consider the smallness of Things.

An "Atom" is the *chemical* unit of Substance—that is, the smallest chemical part that can enter into combination. It has been considered indivisible—that is, incapable of further sub-division. That is, it has been so considered, until very recently, but the latest discoveries have exploded this idea, and have shown the Atom is composed of certain other Things, as we shall see a little later on. Still we may use the Atom as a very good unit of measurement, for it still represents the unit of *chemical* Substance, just as the molecule is the unit of *physical* Substance. In order that you may understand the difference between Molecules and Atoms—physical units, and chemical units, let us give you a few examples.

Take a molecule of water—the *physical* unit, you remember. When it is chemically separated or analyzed, it is found to contain two atoms of hydrogen, and one atom of oxygen—both chemical units, remember—which when united and combined, form water, but which when separated are simple atoms of certain chemical gases. The proportion in water is always the same, two of hydrogen and one of oxygen—this is the only partnership that will form water. The molecule of table salt contains one atom of sodium and one of chlorine. The molecule of air contains five chemical gases, of which nitrogen and oxygen are the principal ones, the proportion being about three parts of nitrogen to one of oxygen. Some molecules are far more complex, for instance the molecule of sugar is composed of *forty-five* chemical atoms, and sulphuric acid of seven. An atom is estimated at one-250,000,000th of an inch in diameter.

But this is not all. The old theory of the finality, and ultimateness of the Atom has been shattered by the recent discoveries of Science. The atom of Hydrogen was formerly considered to be the refinement of Substance—the Ultimate Atom—the smallest and finest Atom possible or known—the last thing that could be imagined about Substance. Some even went so far as to declare that the Atom of Hydrogen was the Ultimate Element, that is the Element out of which all other atoms were made—the mother of Atoms—the Origin of Substance. It was supposed that all other Atoms of Matter were composed of a varying number of hydrogen Atoms, which themselves were "vortex-rings in the Ether"—and that analysis could go no further. Science rested on its oars, and pronounced the work of a century completed.

But alas! no sooner was this position reached, than the discovery of Radiant Matter and the formulation of the "Corpuscle Theory" brought down the whole theoretical structure, and Science was compelled to take up the hunt again, and to probe further into the inner recesses of Things for the Ultimate Thing. But, nevertheless, Atoms still exist, although their finality is no longer urged. The facts remain, although the theory has fallen.

Let us see about this latest theory—the Corpuscle or Electron Theory. The discovery of Radiant Matter, and the investigation of the late discovery of Radium, has led to the further discovery that each Atom, instead of being a "thing-in-itself" is a little mass containing numerous other "Things" called "Corpuscles" (or "Electrons," because electrified). The theory is this, briefly: That each Atom is a minute mass of Substance containing a number of "electrified particles," which are known as Electrons, in constant motion and vibration, revolving around each other, as do the planets, suns, and moons of the Universe—in fact each chemical Atom is like unto a Universe in itself. The simplest Atom—that which was supposed to be the "Ultimate Atom"—the Atom of Hydrogen—is supposed to contain within its tiny self no less than 1,000 minute Corpuscles, which because electrified are called "Electron," revolving in fixed and regular orbits within the containing globe of the Atom. The more complex forms of Atoms are supposed to contain a far greater number of Electrons, the authorities estimating those in an Atom of Oxygen at 10,000; those in an Atom of Gold, 100,000; and those in an Atom of Radium, 150,000. These figures are of course mere "scientific guesses" but when compared with the similar "guess" regarding the size of the Atom, they give a startling illustration of the size of the newly discovered Corpuscle or Electron.

Another authority, for an illustration, asks us to consider a great globe about 100 feet in diameter—that is, of course, 100 feet through its centre. Let the globe represent the Atom. Then imagine 1,000 minute "specks," each the size of a pin-point, composed of Substance, and each containing, as in a capsule, an atom of electricity. Each "speck" is revolving around each other in a regular orbit, in that great "100 feet through" globe, and keeping well away from one another. That will give you an idea of the relative size of the Electrons and Atoms, and the room that the former have to move about in—good many feet between each, you will notice. Lots of room, and plenty to spare. Try to figure out the size of an Electron.

Many readers of the magazines have been confused as to the relation between the Corpuscles and the Electrons (or Ions, as some have called the latter.) The matter is very simple. They are both the same. The Corpuscle is the tiny particle of Matter, which because it is electrified and has thus become the "unit of electricity," is called an "Electron." From the viewpoint of Substance we call the tiny particle a "Corpuscle"—from the viewpoint of Electricity, we call it an "Electron."

These Electrons are the tiny particles that pour forth from the pole in the Crookes' Tube, and constitute what are known as "X Rays," "Cathode Rays," "Becquerel Rays," etc. They also are the particles that are thrown off and emitted by Radium, and similar substances. They exist in the Atom, as explained, but also are found "free" and independent, and in the last condition or state are thrown off in the aforesaid "Rays," and by Radium, etc. So far the Corpuscles are known only as charged with Electricity, and the Electron only as a tiny charge of Electricity with which the Corpuscle is charged. But Science dreams of Corpuscles of Substance other than Electrons, in which case the old Occult teachings of "light dust" and "heat dust," etc., will be verified.

The Electron contains a powerful charge of Electricity, as much in fact as an Atom, 1,000 to 150,000 times its size will carry. But Science is wondering how these highly charged particles manage to hold together in the Atom, so rigidly coherent as to appear indestructible. We think that we may get a hint at the matter a little later on in this book.

Science, or at least *some* scientists, are wondering whether the "whirl" or vibration of the Corpuscle might not produce that which we call "Electricity," and whether, when this motion is intensified, waves of Electricity will not be emitted. The writer fully agrees with this idea, and finds that it fits closely his own theories regarding Substance and Motion. But the reader is cautioned against falling into the error of many recent popular writers on the subject, some of whom have used terms calculated to convey the idea that the Corpuscle (Electron) is Electricity *itself*, rather than tiny particles of Substance called Corpuscles, charged with the unitary charge of Electricity, and therefore called "Electrons." But for that matter, Electricity is only known to us as associated with some form of Substance, and not as "a thing-in-itself." We shall see the reason for this as we proceed with this book. These Corpuscles are destined to play a most important part in the theories of Science from now on. They already have overturned several very carefully and laboriously erected theoretical structures—and many more will follow, among the many important ones evidently doomed to the dust-heap being the "vortex-ring" atomic theory, and other theories built upon the Etheric origin of Matter, and other theories concerning the Ether, even to the extent of breaking down the theory of The Ether itself, which theory had almost come to be considered a Law.

We shall further consider the Corpuscles, and their qualities, characteristics, etc., in the next chapter, for they have an important bearing upon the theories advanced in the course of the study of this book.

CHAPTER-VI

Substance And Beyond

SCIENCE has ascribed to Substance certain characteristic qualities which it calls "Properties." It divides these properties into two classes, *viz.*: (1) Molecular Properties (sometimes called Physical Properties); and (2) Atomic Properties (sometimes called Chemical Properties).

Molecular Properties are those which may be manifested by Substance without disturbing the Molecules, and consequently without affecting the "kind" of Substance.

Atomic Properties are those which concern the Atoms when free from Molecular combination, and which consequently cannot be manifested without changing the "kind" of Substance.

Science, before long, is likely to add a third class of Properties, namely, "*Corpuscular Properties*," relating to the Corpuscles or particles of Radiant Matter, but, so far, it has not had the opportunity to sufficiently observe these qualities, except in a general way

There are certain General Properties that seem possessed by both Mass, Molecules, and Atoms—and probably by Corpuscles.

These *General Properties* are as follows:

Shape: That property whereby Substance "takes up room." This property manifests in three directions, called Dimensions of Space, namely, Length, Breadth, and Thickness.

Weight: That property whereby Substance responds to Gravity. Weight is simply the measure of the attraction.

Impenetrability: That property whereby two bodies of Substance are prevented from occupying the same space at the same time. A nail driven into a piece of wood, simply pushes aside the molecules, and occupies the Space between them. Substance is never actually "invaded" or its actual territory occupied by other Substance.

Indestructibility: That property whereby Substance is prevented from being destroyed or annihilated. Although the forms of Substance may be changed, or transformed into other forms, still, Substance *in itself* is not destroyed, and cannot be under the existing Laws of the Universe.

Mobility: That property whereby Substance responds to imparted Motion. We shall notice this property in our consideration of Motion. In addition to the Motion of the Mass, and the movements of Molecules and Atoms in response to its Attraction, there is another form of Motion constantly going on, without reference to the Attraction or impressed Motion of the Mass. The Molecules of all bodies are always in a state of rapid Motion, called Vibration. In solids this vibration is short, being restrained by the close cohesive position of the Molecules. But in Liquids, the Molecules being further separated, the vibration is far more rapid, and they move around and slide over each other with comparatively little resistance. In gases and vapors the Molecules have a splendid field for Motion, and consequently vibrate in wide fields and orbits, and dash around with the greatest velocity. The Atoms also are believed to vibrate rapidly, in accordance with their own laws of vibration. And the Corpuscles are believed to far excel the last two mentioned particles in intensity, rapidity and complexity of their vibrations, as we shall see a little later on in the book. All Substance is in constant Motion and Vibration. There is no Rest in Substance.

Inertia: That property whereby Substance may not move unless in response to imparted Motion; nor terminate its Motion, when it is once imparted, except in response to some other manifestation of impressed Force. Science holds that this "impressed Force" or "imparted Motion" must come from without, but the writer holds that Force may also be "expressed" from "within," as may be seen by reference to subsequent chapters of this book.

Attraction: That property whereby particles or bodies of Substance (1) draw other particles or bodies toward themselves; or (2) move toward other particles or bodies; or (3) are mutually drawn together. This property manifests in four forms, generally referred to as separate and distinct from each other, but which the writer believes to be but forms of the same Attractive Power, and which he believes to be a Mental Process, at the last analysis (a revolutionary claim, which will be supported by argument in later chapters of the book). These three forms of Attraction are known as (1) Gravitation; (2) Cohesion; (3) Adhesion; and (4) Chemical Affinity, or Chemism. We are invited to consider them briefly, at this point, further investigation being reserved for our chapters on Motion, and Dynamic Thought.

Gravitation: This term is usually applied to the attraction between Masses of Substance, such as the Sun, the Earth, and Masses of Substance on or about the Earth's surface. However, Newton, who discovered the facts of Gravitation, states the Law, as: "*Every particle of matter in the Universe, attracts every other particle," etc.*

Cohesion: This term is used to indicate the attraction between Molecules, by which they are combined into Masses or Bodies. Cohesion causes the Molecules to unite and cling together, thus forming the Mass.

Adhesion: This term is used to indicate the attraction between Masses which causes them to "stick together" without a cohesion of their Molecules. Adhesion operates through the adjacent surfaces of the two Masses. It may be considered as a "lesser" form of cohesion.

Chemical Affinity (sometimes called Chemism or Atomic Attraction): This term is used to indicate the attraction between the atoms, by which they combine, unite and cling together, forming the Molecule.

Science has before it the task of naming, and classifying, the attraction between the Corpuscles, by which they combine and form the Atom. But whatever the name, it will be seen that it represents but another manifestation of "Attraction."

Arising from Molecular Attraction, or Cohesion, are several "Properties" peculiar to Masses having Molecules, and resulting from the tendency of the latter to resist separation. We had better consider them briefly, in order to understand the power of Molecular Attraction, and its incidents.

Porosity: That property indicating the distances observed by the Molecules in their relation to each other, which varies in different "kinds" of Substance. All Substance is more or less Porous, that is, has more or less space existing between the Molecules—the degree depends upon the "closeness." Compressibility and Expansibility, sometimes mentioned as "properties," are but results of Porosity.

Elasticity: That property whereby bodies resume their original size and form, after having been compressed, expanded or "bent." The result is caused by the inclination of the molecules to resume their original positions. What is sometimes called "Plasticity" is merely the reverse of Elasticity, and denotes a limited degree of the latter.

Hardness: That condition resulting from Molecular Attraction resisting the forcible entrance and passage of other Substance between the molecules.

Tenacity: That condition resulting from Molecular Attraction resisting the forcible pulling asunder, or tearing apart of the Mass. This condition sometimes is called "Toughness."

Malleability: That condition resulting from Molecular Attraction resisting the forcible separation of the Mass by pounding, hammering or pressure. The resistance is "passive," and consists of the Molecules allowing themselves to assume a spread-out formation, rather than to be forced apart.

Ductility: That condition resulting from Molecular Attraction resisting the forcible separation of the Mass by a "drawing out" process. The resistance is "passive," and consists of the Molecules allowing themselves to be drawn out into a formation of the shape of wire or thread, rather than to be pulled apart.

In any of the above cases, we may intelligently, and with propriety, substitute the words, "*Molecules, by means of cohesion, resisting, etc.*," for the terms above used, "Molecular Attraction, resisting, etc."

All Masses of Substance (probably Molecules as well) are capable of *Expansion and Contraction*, both phenomena, in fact, and in degree, resulting from the relation of the Molecules. Contraction is a "crowding together" of the Molecules; Expansion a "getting apart" of them.

Density: The amount of Substance in relation to a given bulk. *Volume*—the "size" or "bulk" of a body of Substance. *Mass*—Besides being used to designate a "body" of Substance, composed of two or more Molecules, the term "Mass" is used to designate the "total quantity of Substance in a Body." An application of the above terms may be seen in the following illustration:

A quart of water occupies a certain space—and has a certain "volume," "mass" and "density." Convert the same "mass" of Water into Steam, and it expands to a "volume" of 1700 times that of Water—but, as no molecules have been added, the "mass" remains the same—but as a quart of Steam weighs 1700 times less than the same "volume" of Water, the "density" of Steam is 1700 times less than that of Water. As the "volume" of a given "mass" increases, the "density" decreases in the same proportion—but the "mass" remains the same. "Mass" therefore has two factors, *i.e.*, "Volume" and "Density." The "Density" of a "Mass" is determined by the *weight* of a certain "Volume" of it.

The above consideration of the "Properties" of Substance dealt only with the Molecular Properties, or Physical Properties, as they are sometimes called—that is, with properties depending upon the existence of the Molecules. When we consider the Molecules as being composed of Atoms, and when we consider the processes whereby these Molecules are built up of, or broken down through the separation of Atoms, we come to the subject of Atomic Properties, or Chemical Properties, as they are often called.

The Atomic Properties of Substance consist principally in the power and manifestation of Motion, in the direction of combination, separation, and the complex motions resulting from the same. This Motion is manifested by reason of Atomic Attraction, sometimes called "Chemical Affinity," which we shall consider a little later on in the chapter.

Atomic Principles, as above mentioned, are best illustrated by a reference to Chemical changes, and we shall now examine the same. And, the better way to consider Chemical Changes is by comparing them with Physical Changes, or Changes of the Molecules.

Some Physical Changes in Substance are brought about by Heat, which tends to separate the molecules, or rather to allow them to spread out away from each other, so long as the high temperature is maintained, the degree of their nearness being influenced by temperature. Other Physical Changes are produced by outside Forces separating the molecules to such an extent—to such a distance—that their cohesive force is lost, and the Solid matter is said to be "broken," or even reduced to dust. Other physical changes are brought about by Electricity, causing the Molecules to separate and disintegrate.

Chemical Changes, as distinguished from Physical Changes, do not involve or deal with Molecules, the action being solely upon the Atoms of which the Molecules are composed. Physical Changes *separate* Molecules from each other, while Chemical Changes destroy and break up the Molecule, so that its identity is forever lost, its Atoms thereafter either existing free from combinations, or else recombining with other Atoms, and forming new combinations. Chemical changes are occasioned by either physical or chemical agencies. The physical agencies generally employed are heat, electricity, light, pressure, percussion, etc. The principle of Chemical Changes is that the Atoms are possessed of, and subject to, what is called "Atomic Attraction" or "Chemical Affinity," which may be defined as an attraction or "love" existing in varying degrees between Atoms. This Affinity causes Atoms of one element to seek out and ally themselves to Atoms of another element, the element of "choice" or "preference" being strikingly in evidence.

Atoms of different elements form marriages, and cling together in harmony, until, perchance, by some physical or chemical agency, the Molecule is brought in sufficiently close connection with another Molecule composed of different elemental atoms, when, alas! one of the Atoms of our Molecule finds that it has a greater Affinity for some other elemental Atom in the second Molecule, and lo! it flies away, leaving its first partner, and seeking the new charmer. Divorce and re-marriage is a common thing in the world of Atoms—in fact, Chemistry is based upon these qualities.

Physical and Chemical Changes gradually transform solid rock to "earth" or "soil." Disintegration, by the action of changes in temperature, rains and atmospheric influences, and other Physical Changes, have slowly worn down the rocks into "dirt," gravel, clay, loam, etc. And Decomposition by Chemical Change that set the atoms free from their combinations has aided in the work.

There is no rest in the world of Substance. Everything is changing—constantly changing. Old forms give way to new, and these, grown old while being born, are, in turn replaced by still newer. And on, endlessly. Nothing persists but change. And yet nothing is destroyed, although countless forms and shapes have succeeded each other. Substance is always there, undisturbed and unaffected by the varieties of forms it is compelled to undergo. Masses may change—and do change. Molecules may change—and do change. Disintegration and decomposition affect both, and bring to them the death of form. But their substance endures in the Atom. Atoms may change, and decompose, or undergo whatever change that is their fate, and still the Corpuscles, or what lies beyond the Corpuscles will remain. The Atom was once regarded as Eternal, but now even it seems to be capable of dissolving into some finer division of Substance—and perhaps still finer subdivisions await it.

That familiar form of Substance that we call "earth," "dirt," "soil," etc., is but the result of disintegrated rock, which has crumbled and lost its former form through the action of air, water and atmospheric influences. And the rocks themselves, from which the "soil" came, were at one time a sea of melted, flowing liquid Substance, somewhat resembling volcanic lava. And this "melted rock" is thought to have been condensed from the same principles in the shape of vapor, that existed in the early days of our planetary system. Vapor, gas, liquid, semi-liquid, solid rock, "soil"—the Substance unchanged, the forms totally unlike. Helmholtz estimates the density of the nebulous vapors of Substance as being so rare that it would take several millions of cubic miles of it to weigh a single grain. Oh, Nature, what a wizard thou art!

We have spoken of Air and Water, in a former chapter, and their constituent atoms have been named. And from these three great reservoirs of Substance—the Earth, the Air, and the Water—are obtained all the material that goes to form the bodies of the animal and vegetable kingdoms. The plant draws its nourishment from the soil, the air, and water, and in its wonderful chemical laboratory is able to transform the elements so drawn from these sources into a substance called "Plasm," which consists principally of carbon, oxygen, nitrogen and hydrogen, being nearly identical in composition to the white of an egg, and which constitutes the basis of animal and plant bodily structures. All the material of the physical bodies, of men, animals and plants, are but forms of Plasm. The animals, and man, obtain their nourishment, directly or indirectly, from the plant body, and so at the last we are seen to draw from the soil, air and water all our bodily nourishment, which we convert into bodily structure, bone, muscle, flesh, blood, veins, tissue, cells, etc. And the chemical atoms of our bodies are identical with those in the rock, the air, the water. And so you see the universality of Substance and its countless forms and appearances.

Chemistry resolves Substance back into about seventy-five simple substances, of which Atoms are the Units, which simple substances are called "Elements." From these Elements (by their Atoms) all other substances are formed by combinations, the number of such possible combinations being infinite. An Element (in order to be an element) must be a "simple" substance, that is, must be incapable of further analysis into some other elements. The seventy-five elements, now recognized by science, have never been resolved into other elements, by chemical analysis, and therefore are accepted as "simple." But, it is true that other substances that were formerly considered as simple elements were afterward decomposed by electricity, and found to consist of two or more simpler substances or elements. Thus new elements were discovered, and old ones discarded as "not-elemental." And this fate may be in store for a number of the elements now on the list—and many new ones may be discovered.

For a long time Science was endeavoring to trace all elements back to Hydrogen, the latter being considered the "Ultimate Element," and its atoms composing all the other atoms, under varying conditions, etc. But this theory is now almost abandoned, and Science rests on its list of seventy-five elements, the atoms of which are composed of "Electrons."

Some have hazarded the theory that the Elements were all forms of Ether (see next chapter), their apparent differences resulting merely from the varying rate of vibration, etc. And, in fact, such theory was about finally adopted as a working hypothesis until the discovery of the Corpuscle. Everything in Substance now seems to be moving back to the Corpuscle, as we shall see a little further on.

The following is a list of the principal Elements, known to Science, to-day:

Aluminum.

Antimony.

Arsenic.

Barium.

Bismuth.

Boron.

Bromine.

Cadmium.

Calcium.

Carbon.

Chlorine.

Chromium.

Cobalt.

Copper.

Fluorine.

Gold.

Hydrogen.

Iodine.

Iron.

Lead.

Magnesium.

Manganese.

Mercury.

Nickel.

Nitrogen.

Oxygen.
Phosphorus.
Platinum.
Potassium.
Radium.
Silicon.
Silver.
Sodium.
Strontium.
Sulphur.
Tin.
Zinc.

Of the above, Hydrogen is by far the lightest in weight; in fact it is used as a unit of Atomic Weight, its weight being marked "1" on the scale; Gold, 197; Lead, 207; Silver, 108; Oxygen, 16; Nitrogen, 14; Iron, 56.

The discovery of the Corpuscle, or Electron, rudely shattered the vortex-ring theory of the origin of the Atom, and now, instead of the Atom being regarded as a "vortex-ring" in that hypothetical, paradoxical absurdity, the Ether, it is believed to be composed of a vast number of tiny particles called Corpuscles, as we saw stated in our last chapter. These Corpuscles seem to be the "last thing in Substance"—its last known state of refinement, and already it is being proclaimed as the long-sought for "Primal Matter," or "Ultimate Substance." Whether or not a still finer state of Substance will be discovered Science is unable to say, but thinks it unlikely. But we must not overlook the old Occult Teaching indicating a state of Substance so fine that it is imperceptible, and only recognizable as apparently "free force"; its covering, or vehicle of Substance not being evident. This would seem to indicate a still further refinement of Substance, although perhaps the "Corpuscle" or "Electron" will answer to "fill the bill" in the case.

As to the Corpuscle being "Primal Substance," it must be admitted that its advocates have presented a very strong case. One of their most important points is that although Molecules differ very materially from each other, according to their kinds; and while Atoms likewise manifest very plainly their "kind," the Corpuscle seems to possess *only one "kind,"* no matter from what form or "kind" of Substance it is thrown off. Just think what this means. It means that the finest particles of Gold, Silver,

Iron, Hydrogen, Oxygen, and all the rest of the Elements, *are composed of identically the same material, and exhibit no differences in "kind."* The Elements are no longer "Simple." *All Substance is One, at the last analysis!*

The Corpuscles seem to possess the same Mass—to carry the same charge of Electricity—to act precisely the same—irrespective of their source. No difference in size, mass or character, as in the case of the Atom—all are identical, save in the rate of their vibration at the time of observation, which is simply a matter of more or less Motion. Space seems to be flooded with these tiny particles—these Units of Substance. They stream from the Sun; the Stars; and every body highly heated. Likewise they stream from the bodies of highly electrified Substance. Groups of these Corpuscles, absolutely identical in nature, size, mass, etc., constitute the Atoms of the Seventy-five Elements, the "kind" of Element seemingly being dependent upon the number and arrangement of the Corpuscles, and possibly by their rate of vibration. Every Atom is like a great bee-hive with a swarm of Corpuscles vibrating, moving around each other, and upon their own centres. And, if by the action of intense heat, transmitted, or caused by interrupted Motion—or if by a strong Electric charge—some of these Corpuscles are detached from the Atoms (or possibly an Atom broken up), they fly off through Space at a marvellous speed of many thousand miles an hour.

So we see that these wonderful Corpuscles look very much like Primal Matter or Ultimate Substance—the "Stuff" out of which Substance is made. And, taking you back to the chapter on "The Universality of Life and Mind," the writer would remind you that in their Motions and evident Attraction, etc., these Corpuscles evidence the same "Life and Mind" that we observed in the Molecules and Atoms. It must be so, for what is in the manufactured article must be in the material of which the article is made. And so, even here, Life and Mind have not escaped us. Nor will it in The Ether!

And speaking of the Corpuscles, as "manufactured articles," we are reminded of Herschel's thought about the Atoms, when they were regarded as Primal Matter and likely to be uniform, and, at the end, of one primal substance. Although Herschel's conception does not now apply to the Atoms, it may be transferred to the Corpuscles.

Herschel thought that the fact that the Particles of Substance were likely to be found to be uniform in size, and identical in nature and characteristics, indicated that they might be akin to "manufactured articles," turned out from the same great machinery of Creation. This idea would indicate that the Creator applied the rules of careful manufacture to the manufacture of the Particles, the uniformity operating in the direction of (1) Economy of Material; (2) Utility through interchangeability, replacing broken or discarded parts, etc.; and also (3) Conformity to a Standard of Size, Quality, etc.

The thought is interesting, and is mentioned here for that reason. It is not affected by the supposition that there may be a still finer and rarer form of Substance, from which the Particles are "manufactured"—in fact, the idea of Herschel, if closely analyzed, would seem to indicate some such "raw material" from which the articles were manufactured.

CHAPTER-VII
The Paradox of Science

IN the days of the ancients, when the philosophers found themselves unable to account for any particular class of phenomena, they bundled it together and referred it to a suppositious Something that they called "The Ether." Finding this an easy way to get rid of vexatious questions, they fell into the custom—and the habit grew upon them. Soon there were a dozen or more different kind of Ethers in vogue, each explaining something else—the "something else," by the way, being things that Science *now* feels that it understands pretty well. These Ethers grew to be like the various "Vapors" of the ancients—a dignified term for "We don't know"—a respectable road for retreat under the semblance of an advance.

These Ethers became a scientific scandal, and caused a lax mode of thinking among students of those times. And so they were finally abolished and relegated to the scrap pile of Science, where they lay for many centuries until a comparatively recent period, when at least one of them was hauled forth, dusted, freshened up a little, and placed upon its old pedestal. This revamped Ether, referred to, was the "Ether of Aristotle." Aristotle, as we know, was a famous Greek philosopher who lived about 350 *b.c.*—about 2250 years ago. He was a good man and a celebrated philosopher, but was somewhat deficient in scientific knowledge. Although he knew many things, and uttered many wise thoughts, he was under the impression that the breath of Man entered the heart instead of the lungs—that the back part of the skull was empty, and so on. He was without the advantages of a modern training—which, was not his fault, however.

Well, Aristotle conceived the idea of an Universal Ether, which he thought pervaded all space, and with which he accounted for the passage of light from the sun and stars; the movements of the planets, and various other physical phenomena. It is not known whether Aristotle really *believed* in this Ether, or whether he merely used it as a speculative hypothesis, following the Ether Habit of his contemporaries. At any rate, his theory served its purpose—lived, flourished, declined and died—at least seemed to be dead. But its corpse was resurrected in modern times, and used to account for divers things.

This does not mean that modern thinkers really "believe" in the Universal Ether—they merely assume it as a working hypothesis until something better is offered.

Its principal modern use is to account for the transmission of Light from the Sun and Stars to the Earth. It was held that a thing could not act "where it was not," and so it became necessary to account for the transmission either by the theory that small particles of substance were thrown off from the Sun, and travelled to the Earth, or else that there was some medium of communication by means of vibrations, etc. Newton held to the first theory, but his hypothesis went down before the Ether advocates, who advanced the "wave-theory," although it seems that, like Banquo's ghost, Newton's theory will not stay down, and is now taking on a new lease of life, owing to the discovery of the Corpuscle and Radiant Matter.

The Wave-theory philosophers asserted that the Light and Heat of the Sun were thrown off in the shape of Force or Energy, and transformed into "waves" in and of a hypothetical Ether (Aristotle's own), which waves were carried to the Earth, where, meeting Substance, they were again transformed into Heat and Light.

It was known that Light and Heat travelled at the rate of 184,000 miles per second, and therefore the "waves" of the Ether were considered to have that speed. The Wave-theory seemed to fit the facts of the case better than the Newtonian Theory of Corpuscles, although the latter has always been considered as better explaining certain phenomena than the new theory. And so the Ether Wave became generally accepted, and remains so to-day, although recent discoveries are causing a disturbance in the scientific camp regarding the question.

Later it was discovered that the Electricity travelled at the same rate as Light and Heat, and the Wave-of-the-Ether theory was thus thought to have additional verification, and Electricity came under the Law and remained there until the Electron discovery, which is causing much disturbance, among those interested in the study of Electricity.

Briefly stated, the theory of the Universal Ether is this:

That pervading all Space in the Universe—not only between planets, stars and suns, but also "filling in the cracks" between molecules, and atoms as well—there is a subtle Substance in and through which the waves of Light, Heat, Electricity and Magnetism travel at the rate of 184,000 miles per second. This Substance is said to be "Matter that is not Matter"—in fact, Science does not venture to say just *what* it is, although it freely states just what some of its properties must be, and, alas! these properties are most contradictory and opposite to each other, as we shall see as we proceed.

This Universal Ether is purely hypothetical. It has been called a "necessity of Science"—something assumed for the purpose of explaining or accounting for certain phenomena. It is undemonstrated and unproved—in fact, may truthfully be said to be undemonstrable and unprovable. Some have gone so far as to say that its claimed properties and qualities render it "unthinkable" as well. And yet, Science finds itself compelled to assume that the Ether, or "something like it" exists, or else cease speculating about it. It belongs to the realm of pure theory, and yet, many writers treat it as if it were a positively demonstrated and proven fact. Let us examine into the nature of Science's problem, and her attempted solution, and the trouble arising therefrom.

Light travels at the rate of 184,000 miles a second. Remember, that Light and Heat are that which we call by those names only when considered in connection with Substance. According to the theory, Light in the Sun's atmosphere is transformed into a Light-wave of the Ether on its travels to the earth, and only when the "wave" comes in contact with the Substance on the earth's body or atmosphere does it become again transformed into Light as we know it. In its travels through space it meets with no Substance, and has nothing to "turn into light"—consequently Space (between worlds) is in a state of absolute darkness. The same is true of Heat, and inter-world Space is absolutely cold, although passing through it are countless heat-waves of great intensity, which, later on, will be transformed into Heat when they reach the Substance, the earth. The same is true of Electricity and Magnetism.

Although the Ether, as we have seen, is a purely theoretical substance, yet Science has found it reasonable to conclude that it must be possessed of certain attributes in order to account for certain known facts. Thus, it is said to be frictionless, else the worlds, suns and planets could not pass freely through it, nor could the light and heat waves travel at such a tremendous rate. It also is thought to have something like Inertia, because Motion once started in it persists until stopped; because it is at a state of rest until Motion is imparted to it; and because it takes a fraction of time to impart motion to it. It is thought to be different from Substance in any of its known forms, for many reasons, among such being the fact that no known form of Substance could carry vibrations through space at the rate of 184,000 miles a second. And Light and Heat waves travel at that rate, and have forms and shapes, and lengths of their own. Light for instance, vibrates on two planes, and a light-wave is something like a Greek cross, thus (- | -), having a horizontal and a vertical line, or plane of vibration. And the Ether cannot be a fluid of any degree, because a fluid cannot transmit cross vibrations at all. And it cannot be a Solid, because a Solid could not stand vibrations at such a terrific speed, and still remain a Solid. And yet, to transmit the two-plane light waves, the Ether must have a certain degree of Rigidity, else the waves could not travel. Lord Kelvin estimated this degree of Rigidity as about 19,000,000,000th of the rigidity of the hardest steel. So, you see, Science is compelled to assume that the Ether is "a continuous, Frictionless medium, possessing both Inertia and Rigidity." Some scientists have thought it to be a kind of "elastic jelly."

Of the Ether, Prof. Oliver Lodge has said, "We have to try and realize the idea of a perfectly continuous, subtle, incompressible substance, pervading all Space, and penetrating between the molecules of ordinary Matter, which are imbedded in it, and connected to one another by its means. And we must regard it as the one universal medium by which all actions between bodies are carried on. This, then, is its function—to act as the transmitter of motion and energy."

To give you an idea of the wonderful thing that Science is compelled to think of the Ether as being, by reason of the qualities it is compelled to ascribe to it—although it confesses itself unable to "imagine" the nature of the "Thing" which it has created in bits by the adding and bestowing of qualities which were made necessary by the logical requirements of the case—let us take a hurried view of the Thing as the several departments of Science say it must be thought of.

To meet the requirements of the case, Science says that The Universal Ether must be Substance infinitely more rare and evanescent than the finest gas or vapor known to Science, even in its rarest condition. It must convey Heat in the manner of an infinitely Solid body—and yet it must not be a Solid. It must be transparent and invisible. It must be Frictionless, and yet Incompressible. It cannot be a Fluid. It cannot have Attraction for Substance, such as all Substance has. Nor can it have Weight—that is, it is not subject to Gravitation. It is beyond the reach of any known scientific instrument, even of the greatest power, and it refuses to register itself in any way, either to senses or instruments.

It cannot be known "of itself," but may only be recognized as existent by the "things" for which it acts as a medium or transmitting agent. It must convey Energy and Motion, yet it must not take up any part of either from the Matter in its midst. It must not absorb any of the Heat, Light or Electricity. It must fill up the spaces between the worlds, as well as the most minute space between the Molecules, Atoms and Corpuscles, or any other minute particle of Substance, either known by name to Science now or which may be discovered or imagined later as a necessity of some conception regarding the nature of Substance. In short, The Universal Ether, in order to do the things attributed to it, must be more solid than Solids; more Vapor-like and Gas-like than Vapor or Gas; more fluid than Fluids; infinitely less rigid than steel, and yet infinitely stronger than the strongest steel. It must be a substance having the qualities of a vacuum. It must be continuous and not composed of Particles, Atoms or Molecules. It must be an "everything" in some respects, and yet a "nothing" in others. It must not be Substance, and yet it must carry Substance within its ocean of dimensions, and, besides, interpenetrate the most minute space between the particles of Substance. It must not be Energy or Force, and yet Science has been considering Energy and Force as but "interruptions of rest" or "agitations" within, and of, itself.

So you see that this mysterious, wonderful Universal Ether—in order to "be" at all—must be a "Something" possessing certain qualities or properties of Substance—many of the properties of qualities being exactly contradictory and opposed to each other—and yet it cannot be Substance as we know it. It is a Paradoxical thing. It could only belong to another and an entirely different order of existence from that of Substance as we know it. It must possess characteristics and properties of an order as yet unknown to us by name—for which the material world contains no analogy—for which Substance has no analogues. It must be a far more complex thing than is even the most complex thing we call Matter, or that which we call Force or Energy. And yet, it has been claimed that it would explain both—yes, contain within itself the possibility of both.

And yet, in face of what has just been said, the writer must confess, humbly and with a full realization of the enormity of the offence, that he supposes advancing a theory, a little further on in this book that will attempt to identify this Something—this Universal Ether—with a Something else that we know, although not through the senses or by means of instruments. Bear with him kindly, he begs of you, while he proceeds gradually along the path that leads to the theory.

Scientists have compared Substance moving through the Ether as a coarse seive moving through water, the latter making room for the passage of the seive, and then closing up behind it. If this be amended by the idea that the moving seive, while allowing the water to pass through it freely, still carries along with it a thin film of water which clings to the wires of the seive by adhesion—if there be admitted this "clinging film" as well as the body of the water through which the seive moves—then the illustration answers quite well as a crude illustration of Substance and "The Ether." This fact is important in view of the theory that will be advanced, further on in this book. Prof. Lodge, in his interesting work, "Modern Views of Electricity," mentions a number of experiments tending to prove the above mentioned fact, which is not so generally known as other facts relating to the Ether.

Until the discovery of Radiant Matter (bringing with it the new theories of the Corpuscle or Electron, etc.), brushed aside into the dust heap many generally accepted scientific theories regarding the nature of Substance, the favorite and most popular theory was what was known as the "Vortex-ring" theory of the Atom. This theory held that the atoms of Substance were but vortex-rings of the Ether, having had motion communicated to them in some way, and which afterwards acquired other motions, and which finally become apparent to our senses as Substance. In other words, the Atom was supposed to be a vortex-ring of Ether, acted upon by Force, in some unknown way, the character, nature and properties of the Atom being determined by the shape and size of the vortex-ring; the rate of motion; etc., etc.

The new discoveries of Science, however, have set aside (at least temporarily) this "vortex-ring" theory, and at present Science seems to find its "latest thing in Substance," in the theory that Substance—at the last—seems to be the Corpuscle or Electron. In other words, after many years of fancied security in a settled theory regarding the nature of Substance, Science once more finds itself compelled to take up the search for the origin of things. But the theory of the Ether remains—and is likely to—although the names applied to it will change. By some it is still believed that in the Ether, a little further removed, rests the origin of Substance and that the Corpuscle may be the "vortex-ring" product, instead of the Atom.

It will be noticed that Science has made no serious attempt to connect the phenomenon of Gravitation or Attraction with the Ether. Gravitation stands alone—an "outsider" among the Forces, responding to none of their laws—needing no time in which to travel—needing no medium like the Ether in which to transmit "waves"—fearing no obstacle or interfering body, but passing right through the same—different, different, different. And we shall see *why* this difference, when we reach the point where our theory brings us to the point where we must substitute "something else" for that Great Paradoxical General Solvent of Modern Science—the Ether of Aristotle. We shall reach the point after a brief consideration of Motion, Force and Energy.

CHAPTER-VIII

The Forces of Nature

THE Substance filling the Universe is in constant and unceasing Motion. Motion is evidenced in every physical and chemical process and change, and manifested in the constant interchange of position of the Particles of Substance.

There is absolutely no rest in Nature—everything is constantly changing—moving—and vibrating. Building-up processes are ever at work forming larger masses or bodies of the Particles—and tearing-down processes, disintegration and decomposition of Molecules and Atoms, and Corpuscles, are constantly at work also. Nature maintains a constant balance among her Forces. If the building-up energies and forces were allowed full sway, then all the Particles in the Universe ultimately would gravitate to a common centre, thus forming a compact and solid Mass, which would thus dwell for Eternity, unless the Creative Power should move upon it and again scatter its Particles in all directions. And, if the tearing-down, and dispersive forces and energies were allowed full sway, the Particles would fly apart and would remain asunder for Eternity, unless called together by some new Creative fiat.

But Nature pits one force against another, maintaining an equilibrium. The result is constant play and inter-play of forces, causing distribution, and redistribution of Particles, following the gathering-together and building-up processes.

There is no lost motion, or waste force. One form of force and motion is converted into another, and so on, and on. Nothing is lost—all force is conserved, as we shall see as we proceed.

In the public mind—or rather, in the mind of that part of the public which think of the matter at all—there seems to be an idea that "Force" is something of the nature of an entity, separate from Substance or Mind—something that pounces down upon Substance and drives it along by presence from without. The ancient philosophers regarded Substance as acted upon from *without* by an entity called Force, Substance being regarded as absolutely inert and "dead." This idea, which is still held by the average person, owing, doubtless, to the survival of old forms of expression, was generally held by philosophers until the time of Descartes and Newton. This old idea was due to the teachings of Aristotle—he of the Ether Theory—and Science and Philosophy were timid about shaking off the Aristotelian dogmas. Others held that Light, Heat and Electricity were "fluids" conveyed from body to body—in fact the general public still entertains this idea regarding Electricity, owing to the use of the term "the Electric *fluid*."

The present teaching of Science is that Force is the result of the motion of the Particles of Substance, and, of course, originates from *within*, rather than from without. It is true that Motion may be communicated to a body by means of another body in Motion imparting the same to it, but that does not alter the case, for the Original Motion came from the movement and vibration of the Particles of Substance, although it may have passed through many stages of transformation, change and transmission in its progress. The only exception to the rule is Gravitation, which is a form of Force, the nature of which is unknown to Science, although its laws of operation, etc., are understood. We shall learn some new facts about Gravitation in the forthcoming chapters of this book.

It will be well for us to remember *this* fact, in our consideration of Force and Motion—that Force and Motion *originate* from the inherent property of Motion passed by the Particles of Substance, and come from *within*, not from without. This is the best teaching of Modern Science, and also, forms an important part of the Theory of Dynamic Thought which is advanced in this book. Buchner, the author of "*Force and Matter*," vigorously insists upon this conception, saying, among many other similar expressions: "Force may be defined as a condition of activity or a motion of matter, or of the minutest particles of matter or a capacity thereof."

The term "Force" is generally defined in works on Physics as "That which causes, changes or terminates Motion." The word "Force" is generally used in the sense of "in action," while "Energy" is usually used in the sense of "Potential Force—capacity for performing work," the idea being that it is "stored-up" force, or "force awaiting use." The term "Power" is used in two senses, the first meaning "a measure of Mechanical Energy," such as a "forty horse-power engine," etc.; the second sense being "Capacity or Ability to Act, or exercise Force," this use being almost identical to the idea of "Energy," as above described, although, possibly, a little stronger expression.

The Materialistic school holds that Force is a property of Matter, the latter being regarded as the "real thing" of the Universe. Others hold that Force is the "real thing," and that what is called Matter, or Substance, is but a centre of Force, etc. Others hold that the two are but aspects of the same thing, calling the "thing" by the name "Matter-Force," or "Force-Matter." Haeckel calls this combined "thing" by the name of "Substance," claiming that what are called Matter and Force are but "attributes" of it, the third "attribute" being "Sensation," which he holds is akin to Mind—"Haeckel's Substance" is held to be Eternal, and Self-existent—its own Cause, in fact. (In this book the term "Substance" is not used in this sense, but merely as synonymous with what Science usually calls "Matter.")

The views advanced in this book differ materially from any of those above mentioned, it being held by the writer that "All Force is Vital-Mental Force," and, consequently, "Force" as a separate thing is considered an unreasonable proposition—what is called "Force" being considered merely an action of Mind upon Substance, causing Motion. The writer does not intend to advance this idea at this point beyond the mere mentioning of the fact—the theory being brought out and developed as we proceed—and he will proceed to a consideration of the phenomena of Force, along the lines of Modern Science, believing that in this way the subject may be better understood.

The term "Motion," as used in Physics, is defined as: "The act, process or state of changing place or position; movement"—(Webster). So you see, Motion is the movement of Substance changing place or position; Force is that which causes, changes or terminates Motion; and Energy is the "capacity" for manifesting Force; and Power the Ability to Act. In works on Physics you will notice the expression, "Potential Energy," meaning Energy awaiting action; also "Kinetic Energy," meaning Energy in Action; that is, in Motion. We shall not need these terms in this book, but it is well to understand them.

Another term frequently met with, is "Conservation of Energy," which is used to indicate that Law of Physics the operation of which renders Energy indestructible. That is, Science holds that Energy can not be destroyed—that it is not lost, or created, but is merely transformed into other forms of Energy, Potential or Kinetic. Therefore, after Energy is used, it either passes into a state of Potential Energy or Rest, awaiting a future call to Activity, or else is immediately transformed into another form of Kinetic

Energy, or Energy in Action. The theory holds that the quantity or amount of Energy in the Universe is fixed in its totality—none may be created or destroyed—there can be no addition to, or subtraction from the Totality of Energy—that all Energy used has been previously stored up, or else has been immediately transmitted or transformed. It is also held that when Energy manifests as the result of work performed, it is always found that it is at the expense of some previously manifested form of Energy—that the agency by which the work is performed always parts with its stock of Energy, and that the thing worked upon always acquires or gains the amount of Energy lost by the aforesaid agent, or worker—and yet there is no actual loss or gain, but merely transformation.

The above theory is mentioned as of interest in the general subject, although it does not play a prominent part in the subject of this book, for the writer holds that all Energy resides in Mind, and emerges therefrom, and, in the end, returns thereto. This being believed, it is seen that Energy is not to be thought of as a separate thing having a "totality," but merely as a quality of Mind—the question of its totality or fixed quantity not being inquired into, although both, probably, run along the lines of the nature of Mind, and depend upon the limitations, or lack of limitations, of the latter. However, the question does not assume a vital importance in our consideration of the subject.

So far as the question of transmission, or transformation of Energy, is concerned, however, the principles of the Law of Conservation of Energy may be accepted as correct, although it more properly belongs to the principle of what has been called "The Corelation of Force," the idea of which is that one form of Energy may be, and is always, transformed into another form, and so on, and on, unto infinity. This idea is followed in this book, except that the idea of "From Mind originally, to Mind finally," is incorporated within it. This law of the "Corelation of Force" may be illustrated by the following quotation from Tyndall, the great scientist of the last century, who says:

"A river, in descending from an elevation of 7720 feet, generates an amount of heat competent to augment its own temperature 10 degrees F., and this amount of heat was abstracted from the sun, in order to lift the matter of the river to the elevation from which it falls. As long as the river continues on the heights, whether in the solid form as a glacier, or in the liquid form as a lake, the heat expended by the sun in lifting it has disappeared from the universe. It has been consumed in the act of lifting. But, at the moment that the river starts upon its downward course, and encounters the resistance of its bed, the heat expanded in its elevation begins to be restored. The mental eye, indeed, can follow the emission from its source through the ether, as vibratory motion, to the ocean, where it ceases to be vibration, and takes the potential form among the molecules of aqueous vapor; to the mountain-top, where the heat absorbed in vaporization is given out in condensation, while that expended by the sun in *lifting* the water to its present elevation is still unrestored. This we find paid back to the last unit by the friction along the river's bed; at the bottom of the cascade, where the plunge of the torrent is suddenly arrested; in the warmth of the machinery turned by the river; in the spark from the millstone; beneath the crusher of the miner; in the Alpine saw-mill; in the milk-churn of the chalet; in the supports of the cradle in which the mountaineer, by water-power, rocks his baby to sleep. All the forms of mechanical motion here indicated are simply the parcelling out of an amount of calorific motion derived originally from the sun; and, at each point at which the mechanical motion is destroyed or diminished, it is the sun's heat which is restored."

The following quotation, also, is interesting as illustrating another phase of this law:

"The work performed by men and other animals is due to the transformed energy of food. This food is of vegetable origin and owes its energy to the solar rays. The energy of men and animals is, therefore, the transformed energy of the sun. Excepting the energy of the tides, the sun's rays are the source of all the forms of energy practically available. It has been estimated that the heat received by the earth from the sun each year would melt a layer of ice over the entire globe a hundred feet in thickness. This represents energy equal to one horse-power for each fifty square feet of surface."—Anthony and Brackett.

From the above quotations, it will be seen that the principal and most familiar sources (or great storage batteries) of Energy, apparent to dwellers upon this planet, are (1) the Earth manifesting the Power of Gravitation; and (2) the Sun, manifesting solar heat. In Tyndall's illustration we see the force of the sun's Energy—heat—raising the water from the ocean, by evaporation (although aided by the earth's gravitation "pulling down" the heavier air, allowing the vapor to rise). Then we see the Force of Gravitation causes the condensed vapor to fall as rain or snow on the mountain-top—then causing the rain to run into little streams, and so on until the river is reached—then causing the river to start on its downward journey of over seven thousand feet—then causing it to plunge over the cascade; to turn the wheels that operated the machinery, and turned the millstone, and the crusher of the miner, and the saw-mill, and the milk-churn, and the cradle. And, as Tyndall might have added, had he lived a little later—in the running of the dynamo, which running, produced electricity, that in turn caused lights to burn; other machinery to run and manufacture things; stoves to cook; flat-irons to iron; automobiles and engines to run; and many other things along the lines of transmitting Energy, Force and Motion.

And in this consideration, let us not forget the important part that Gravitation—that most wonderful of all Forces—plays in the grand scheme of Nature. Not only does this Force cause the planets to circle around the sun, and, perhaps that sun around another sun, and so on, and on until the matter becomes unthinkable—not only this, but it performs a million parts in the affair of earthly Matter, as we shall see in a later chapter. The Force of Gravitation is one of the greatest mysteries confronting Science to-day, although many believe it a simple question. Gravitation and the Universal Ether contain the great secrets of Nature that Man is striving to unveil. And yet, so "common" is Gravitation that the race, including almost all the scientists, take it as a "matter of course." We shall devote much attention to the question of Gravitation in the forthcoming chapters of this book, for it plays a very important part in the general theory of Dynamic Thought, upon which this book is based. We shall have a special chapter devoted to it, a little later on, and the matter will also come up for explanation further on in the book.

But, in the meantime, let us consider the other forms of Energy, *viz.*, Heat, Light, Magnetism and Electricity, which with Gravitation and Attraction of other kinds, form the Forces of Nature.

CHAPTER-IX
Radiant Energy

THE "kinds" of Energy are very few, although the methods of using, applying and manifesting same are innumerable. Let us begin with one of the best known forms of Energy, namely, Heat.

Heat was formerly regarded as a very fine fluid or substance, called "caloric," which was supposed to enter into Substance and then manifest the phenomenon of "heat." This idea has long since been relegated to the scrap pile of Science. The present theory, which is supported by a mass of evidence obtained through investigation and experimentation, is that Heat is a form of Energy, arising from the vibratory motions of the Particles of Substance—a "Mode of Motion." The degrees of Heat are termed "Temperature." Temperature depends upon the rate of the heat-vibrations of the Particles of Substance, either arising from the Original Motion of the Particles, or else from vibrations or Motion aroused in them by transmission from Particles of other bodies of Substance—these vibrations being "contagious." Temperature then means "the measure of the vibrations of the Particles."

All bodies of Substance have *some* degree of Temperature—some degree of heat-vibration of its Particles. Science has a pleasant "scientific friction" of an Absolute Zero at the degree of 491 below Zero, Fahrenheit, but this is merely an imaginary something with which the grown up children of Science amuse themselves.

When two bodies are brought near each other—the "nearness" being comparative, and, in some cases, meaning a distance of millions of miles—Heat is transmitted from the warmer to the cooler body, until the temperatures are equalized—that is until the two bodies vibrate in unison.

In Physics we are taught that the "Transmission" of Heat may be accomplished in three ways, although the writer is of the opinion that the three ways are but three forms of one way. The first form is called "Conduction," whereby the vibration, or Heat, is conveyed along a body of Substance, from its warmer to its cooler parts—for instance, an iron poker with one end in the fire. The second form is called "Convection," whereby the visible motion of heated Substance, moving along the air—for instance, hot-air, hot-water, steam, etc., either by means of pipes, or by allowing them to pass freely through the air. The third form is called "Radiation," whereby the vibrations are believed to be transformed into "waves of the Ether," which will be spoken of later, in addition to what has been said on the subject in our chapter entitled "The Paradox of Science."

The writer thinks that a little consideration will show us that the same rule operates in all of the above cases, and that "Conduction" and "Convection" are but forms of Radiation. For instance, in Conduction there must be a few Particles first set into vibration, the same gradually passing on to the others farther, and farther away. Passing *how*? "By contact," replies Physics. But, the Particles are never in absolute contact—there always is "plenty of space" between them. And so there must be some kind of "waves" passing through the space between them, which space is not filled with "air," or other form of Substance, but only with "the Ether," or *something that takes its place*. So that, after all, Conduction is but a form of Radiation. And the same rule will apply in the case of Convection.

Heat arises from several causes, all of which, however, manifest through the vibration of the Particles of the body evidencing the Heat. These causes may be stated as (1) Original Motion of the Particles of a body of Substance, arising from some workings of the Law of Attraction, and including Motion arising from Chemical Action, Combustion, etc. (2) From transmission or "contagion" from some other body of Substance, the Particles of which are vibrating at the rate of Heat. (3) From interrupted Motion, including friction both of the moving body with the air or other Substance, and the friction of a current of Electricity passing through the body. In each of the above cases, the *actual* and immediate cause of the Heat is the vibration of the Particles of the Substance manifesting the Heat, although the transmitted vibratory waves, or the interrupted motion, friction, current, etc., may have been the instigator or provoker of such vibration. The interrupted motion, friction, or "wave" does not produce the Heat, but merely arouses or provokes the increased vibration of the Particles, that really manifest the Heat. At the last, remember, the Heat is in the Particles of the body that "feels" or experiences it.

The vibrations of Heat seem to have the properties of causing the Molecules to draw further apart, and to manifest less Attraction, or more Repulsion, whichever way one cares to express it. This "moving away" of the Molecules tend to cause the body to increase in volume or size, and occasions what is known as "Expansion" in Substance. In this way Heat transforms Solids into Liquids; Liquids into Gases or Vapors, the change being wholly a matter of the relative distances of the Molecules.

Magnetism is another form of Energy, and is generally believed to be a part of the phenomena of Electricity, if indeed, not a form of Electricity itself. Science knows very little about the nature of Magnetism, but in a general way holds to the theory that it results from the vibration or motion of the Particles of Substance, as do all other forms of Energy. The magnetic qualities of a body may be increased or decreased by motion affecting the relation of the Molecules, which fact has been regarded as having some bearing on the theory.

Electricity is a form of Energy, that Science regards as also arising from the vibration or motion of the Particles of Substance. It is transmitted, like Heat, by Conduction and Radiation, the "waves" tending to provoke similar vibrations in the Particles of Substances receiving them. By many careful investigators, Electricity is believed to be very closely related to the phenomenon called light, both having much in common. Science seems to be discovering new points of resemblance between them, and it is probable that in the near future they will be seen to be but varying forms of the same thing. The purposes of this book do not call for an extended consideration of the properties of Electricity, the same being served by a consideration of its nature being akin to that of the other forms of Energy, namely, "vibration or motion in or among the Particles of Matter."

Light is a form of Energy, the study of which is of the greatest interest to Science, for the reason that the field seems to be widening out continuously, and reaching out into the territory formerly thought to be the special region of Electricity. And, in another direction, it seems to be reaching out into the territory of Heat, the latter being considered by many to be but a form of Light, in its lower vibrations. In fact, the writer of this book so considers the subject, and for the purposes of this book, in later chapters, he will combine Electricity, Heat, and Light, including, also, the phenomena known as the X-Rays, Becquerel Rays, Radium waves, etc., as forms of Light—the combined forms of Energy to be called "*Radiant Energy*." In this combination, he believes that he is in line with the latest and best thought of Modern Science. However, he does not insist upon his readers following this idea, and so, if they prefer, they may think of each of these forms as separate and distinct, and yet not run contrary to the line of thought of the book.

Light is not the simple thing that it is considered to be by the general public. It is composed of many parts, qualities and manifestations. Its rays, when separated by the Spectrum, are seen to consist of "waves" or vibrations of differing degrees of rate and intensity. The lower range contains the heat rays, and it is interesting to know that there are rays of heat too far down in the scale to be evidenced by human senses that may be distinguished by delicate instruments. But there are rays still further down in the scale that are known to exist, theoretically, that cannot be registered even by the finest instruments. To gain an idea of the delicacy of these instruments, let us remember that Prof. Langley has an instrument called the "Bolometer," that is so delicate that it registers a change of temperature of one millionth of a degree, and will register the heat of a candle one and one-half miles distant from it. Light vibrations arise from combustion, friction, electricity etc., causing the Particles to assume increased Motion.

Let us consider the report of the Spectrum. Beginning with waves or vibrations far below the sensibility of Man, the scale shows an advance until the first "warm" vibration of iron was reached. This first indication of warmth comes when the vibrations reach the rate of 35,000,000,000,000 *per second*. Then gradually they increase until a dull red glow is noticed—the lowest *visible* light ray—when the vibrations are 450,000,000,000,000 per second. Then come the orange rays, then the golden yellow, then the pure yellow, then the greenish yellow, then the pure green, then the greenish blue, then the ocean blue, then the cyanic blue, then the indigo, then the violet—the latter evidencing when the vibrations reach the rate of 750,000,000,000,000 per second. Then come the Ultra-violet rays—invisible to human sight—but evidenced by chemical media. In this Ultra-violet region lies the X-Rays, etc., and also the "Actinic Rays," that produce photographs, sunburn one's face and blister the nose—that cause violent explosions in chemicals—that transform forms of Substance—that are employed to cure skin diseases, etc. These Actinic or Chemical Rays have an important role to play in plant-life, for they act upon the green leaves of the plant, causing a chemical change by which carbonic acid and water are transformed into sugar and starches.

Some of the rays of the Ultra-violet region of Light penetrate substances formerly considered solid and impenetrable. And some of them emitted from Radium, etc., would destroy organic life if applied in sufficient quantities. Some of them are practically waves of Electricity so that Light and Electricity are seen to be closely related.

To give one an idea of the differences produced by different rates of vibration, let us imagine a Mass of Iron, shaped like a great "Top," capable of being impelled to "spin" at a constantly increasing rate of speed, by some Mighty Will. At first it is seen as a slowly spinning Top, manifesting nothing but slow motion, to our senses.

Now, imagine our Top spinning at a rate doubling each second. The first second the Top spins at the rate of two revolutions per second. We notice no change, except that we can see the movement. The next second the revolutions are doubled to four per second. Then, doubling each second, we have, respectively, revolutions of eight per second, then sixteen, and then in the fifth second thirty-two per second. Then we begin to notice a change.

When the revolutions reach thirty-two per second the friction of the moving Top on the air causes it to give forth a very low, deep, bass note of sound. This note is like a low, deep "hum," and is the lowest possible of perception by the human hearing, although it is possible that some of the lower forms of life may be conscious of still lower vibrations.

The sixth second the revolutions reach sixty-four, and the low note has grown much higher in the scale. The seventh second records a rate of 128, and the note has correspondingly increased. Then, as the seconds pass, we have, successively, 256, 512, 1,024, 2,048, 4,096, 8,192, 16,384, 32,768, the latter in the fifteenth second, and representing the highest note recognizable by the human ear, although it is believed that some of the lower animals may recognize sounds too acute for our sense of hearing. During this increase in revolutions from the fifth second to the fifteenth, the sound-note has risen rapidly in the scale from the low sullen "hum," on through the notes of the musical scale, and beyond the range of instruments, until the shrillness becomes so intense as to be almost unbearable, and finally terminating in a shrill, piercing shriek like the "squeak" of the bat, only long-drawn out.

Then from the termination of the sound (by reason of the rate of vibration having become too high) silence reigns for thirty seconds—absolute silence, in spite of the rapidly increasing rate of vibrations, in fact, because of it.

When the forty-fifth second is reached, and the revolutions have reached the rate of 35,184,372,088,832 per second, our Top begins to emit heat-rays, increasing each second. Then a little later a dull, dim glow may be noticed. Then, as the seconds fly, the dull glow manifests a deep dark red color, such as one notices in the iron of the blacksmith's shop, soon after it begins to "glow." Then, on and on, as the seconds fly, the deep red grows lighter and brighter, gradually changing into orange, then into yellow, then into green, then into blue, then into indigo, then into violet, and then into the color of "white-heat." Then this "white-heat" changes into a still more dazzling white, and then a white impossible to describe appears, so bright, clear and brilliant that the eye cannot bear the sight. Then, suddenly, the intense brightness is succeeded by absolute darkness, and the moving Top cannot be seen by the eye—and yet it moves on. The highest recorded chemical rays of light are estimated to equal a rate of vibration of 1,875,000,000,000,000 per second. The vibration of the lowest shade of red light is estimated at 450,000,000,000,000, and the highest of violet at 750,000,000,000,000 per second, so we may imagine what the highest line on the spectrum is like.

Still vibrating, our Top, which has become now a Mass of Vaporized Iron, rapidly tending toward still more ethereal forms. It has passed out from the region of light-waves, into another "Unknown Region" of Vibrations, in which region, however, exist the vibrations known to us as the "X-Rays," etc. It is throwing off great quantities of Electrons. If we were to use a fluorescent screen we would be able to observe the phenomena of the Roentgen Rays, and similar manifestations of Radiant Energy.

On and on vibrates the Top of what we once called Iron—cold iron, warm iron, hot iron, melted iron, gaseous iron, etherealized iron, if you like. What it is like now, the imagination of Man cannot conceive. Still the revolutions continue, doubling each second. *What is being produced?* The imagination cannot conceive of what this state of Substance, now being reached, is like. By a scientific form of poetry we might think of it as melting into Energy—pure Energy, if there were such a thing. Long since it has been resolved into its original Particles—its Corpuscles, and perhaps into the "stuff" from which particles are made. But we must let the curtain drop—the wildest fancy cannot follow the Dance of Substance any further.

The theory of the transmission of vibrations of Radiant Energy by means of "waves" in the Ether, or "something that takes the place of the Ether," has been mentioned in other parts of the book. Referring again to it, the writer would say that he thinks it probable that the "waves" coming in contact with the countless Corpuscles in the Earth's atmosphere, communicate a high rate of motion to them, the result being that they take on the vibrations immediately, and pass along with the "wave" current—the result being that much that we consider as waves of Light, Heat and

Electricity are but streams of these Corpuscles in which vibrations have been awakened by the "waves." This idea will help to explain some of the phenomena of Light, which seemed more understandable under the old Light-Corpuscle theory of Newton than under the "wave" theory of recent years. The idea is advanced merely for the purpose of setting down the thought, for it plays no important part in the theory of the book.

Another matter that should not be overlooked in connection with Light and Heat and Electricity is that Particles absorb or "catch" the vibrations in different degrees, their receptivity depending upon their particular vibratory mode, or "custom of their kind." If unable to "absorb" the vibrations, they "reflect" them. Substance, of any particular kind, absorb Heat in the degree of its atomic weight.

In the next chapter we shall learn something of The Law of Attraction, that wonderful Law that makes possible any Motion or Radiant Energy.

CHAPTER-X
The Law of Attraction

IN the previous chapters we have seen that all forms of Radiant Energy, *viz.*, Light, Heat, Electricity and Magnetism, arose from the Motion of the Particles of Substance. It now becomes important to learn just what cause this "Motions of the Particles." Science is somewhat hazy and foggy on this subject, but in a general way decides that it is caused by "the mutual relations and positions of the particles, arising from their respective attractive qualities," as a recent writer has expressed it. Well, this is better than the old way of seeking refuge and retreat in a mere volume of dense words. It is indeed the only logical conclusion, this one that the operations of the Law of Attraction are manifested in the Motion of the Particles.

This great Law of Attraction is the greatest Law in Nature. It operates on all planes of life. It is always in evidence. Let us consider it.

Let us begin by considering the most magnificent and constant exhibition of that Law—Gravitation. Gravitation is the Riddle of the Universe, and the one form of Energy that balks Science—so much a mystery that Science does not even hazard a "guess" at its nature—no theory of the origin and nature of Gravitation is to be found in "the books." Let us see what Gravitation is.

It is more than the power that "pulls things to the earth," as the average man would define it. It does more than cause water to run down hill, and turn mill-wheels to drive machinery. Water-power results from Gravitation, but even the Energy of Niagara Falls is insignificant when compared to the other manifestations of the Mother of Energy—Gravitation.

Webster defines Gravitation as: "That attraction or force by which all bodies or particles in the universe tend toward each other."

Following that definition, let us add that: *Every particle of Substance has an attraction for every other particle.*

In view of our belief that this "attraction" is a form of mental effort, let us regard the term "Attraction" as being a form of what we call "Desire," or even "Love," in the mental world. If you will think of it in this way, you will be better able to fall in with our lines of thought.

And, in addition to every particle of Substance having an attraction (love or desire) for every other particle, *it has the means and power to draw that other particle toward itself, and to move toward that other particle at the same time.* Webster gives a very clear idea of this when he defines Attraction as: *"An invisible power in a body by which it draws anything to itself; the power in nature acting mutually between bodies, or ultimate particles, tending to draw them together, or to produce their cohesion or combination, and conversely resisting separation."*

The majority of persons, when thinking of "Gravitation," are satisfied with the idea that it is a power that "pulls things down to the ground," and do not think of it as a force that "pulls things" other ways besides "down," and which is possessed and exercised by the speck of dust as well as by the whole earth—by the molecule as well as by the mass. The reason of this is that this power is so slight in small bodies of Substance that it is unnoticed; and that only when the mass is sufficiently large to make the "pull" strong does one perceive and appreciate that the force exists. The lack of information on the part of the average person regarding this subject is amazing, particularly when the importance of the knowledge is understood.

The attraction that holds the molecules of Substance together is Gravitation. The attraction that "pulls" a piece of Substance to the earth is Gravitation. The attraction that keeps the suns and planets in their orbits is Gravitation. Let us see the operations of the Law.

In Astronomy you may learn that the movements of the planets around the sun and the moons around their planets—their regular and constant relative positions—are caused by the force of Gravitation. If it were not for this attraction by the Sun, the planets would fly out into space, like a stone from a sling. The Attraction of Gravitation acts on the planets just as does the string of the whirling sling that keeps the stone from flying away during the whirling until the string is released. Some astronomers think that our sun revolves around some greater sun, and this again around a greater, and so on to infinity. If this be so, then the Attraction of Gravitation is that which holds them all in their orbits and places in spite of their motion.

And in Physics, you may learn that this same Attraction of Gravitation prevents the people and objects on the surface of the earth from flying off into space. And that it holds the portions of the earth together, preventing them from flying apart.

And, remember this, for it is important—the Attraction of the Earth, great and powerful as it is, is nothing more than the *combined* attractive power of its constituent molecules, or atoms, or parts. The centre of the Earth is the Centre of the Attraction, because it is the centre of the aggregation of its Particles.

It must not be supposed that the Earth simply attracts "downward," that is, toward its centre. On the contrary, large masses of earth—large mountains, for instance—exert a certain degree of Attraction of Gravitation, and experiments have shown that a "plumb" is slightly deflected by reason of the proximity of a large mountain. And the reason that bodies "lose weight" as they descend from the surface of the earth is because they leave "above" them a certain large portion of the molecules composing the earth, which mass of molecules exert an attraction proportionate to their mass, which attraction balances the attraction of the mass of earth "beneath them."

Science teaches that if the earth were hollow in the centre, the weight there would be Zero, or nothing at all, and that a body would float in the space at the centre of the earth just as does a balloon in the air, the reason thereof being that the attraction would be equalized—equal attraction from every direction, counterbalancing each other. Considering the earth's radius to be 4000 miles, a body that weighed 100 pounds on the surface would weigh but 75 pounds at the depth of 1000 miles; but 50 pounds at a depth of 2000 miles; but 25 pounds at a depth of 3000 miles; and Nothing, or Zero, at a depth of 4000 miles, which would be the Centre of the Earth. This, of course, supposes that the Substance of which the earth is composed is of uniform density from surface to centre.

From an equal distance above the surface of the earth, bodies released, or dropped, will reach the surface at exactly the same degree of speed, and in exactly the same time—this irrespective of weight or size. In other words, a cork or piece of lead, no matter what their sizes may be, will travel with equal rapidity. In case where the "lighter" substance travels more slowly (compare a feather and bullet, for instance) the difference is caused by the light object meeting with more resistance from the air. This apparent exception has been explained away by the experiment of dropping the bullet and the feather in a vacuum tube, in which there was no resistance from air, the consequence being that both descended precisely at the same instant. Another similar experiment is to place the feather upon a piece of iron whereby the resistance of the air is prevented, and the feather will maintain its position during the drop, and will reach the ground resting on top of the iron, just as it started.

And, remember this please, that the small object attracted by the earth exerts an attraction on its own account. If the two were of the same size they would exert an equal attracting power, but as one is smaller its attracting power is very slight compared with that of the large mass. But it is true that the particle of dust attracts the earth precisely as the earth attracts the particle of dust—the difference being solely a matter of degree depending upon the "mass" of the body. The amount or degree of the *combined* attracting power is determined by the combined total of the two masses. Distance lessens the degree of attraction—thus as bodies are lifted above the earth the weight decreases very gradually, and by very slight degrees, but constantly and invariably. The poles of the earth are flattened, and, consequently, the weight of an object slightly increases as it is carried from equator to pole.

Concluding our consideration of Gravitation, it will be well to call your attention to the fact that Gravitation differs from the forms of Radiant Energy known as Heat, Light, Electricity and Magnetism in several very important particulars, which seems to go far in the direction of proof that the latter are by incidents or consequences of the former.

In the first place, Gravitation, so far as is known, is not dependent upon, caused by, or maintained by, any other Force or form of Energy. Nor does it seem to be derived from some great reservoir, from which it obtains its supply of Energy. On the contrary, it seems to be a "thing-in-itself," self-supporting, self-existing—an intrinsic thing, in fact. It does not seem to be lost to bodies by radiation. And consequently there seems to be no need of a body replenishing its supply, as there is no loss. Gravitation seems to be a constant *something*, remaining always with bodies and neither being lost or acquired. It exists between the Atoms, Molecules, Masses—all in the same way. In fact, one is tempted to think of the planets and worlds in space, as Molecules of some greater Mass held together by Gravitation just as are the Molecules held together. Remember, that the Molecules and Atoms are not in absolute contact, *but there is always a "space" between them*, although the space or distance may be "insensible" to us. "As above, so below," says the old occult aphorism, and it seems to be so.

Then again, Gravitation is believed to act *instantaneously*, and does not require Time to pass between bodies, as does Light, Heat, Electricity, Magnetism—Radiant Energy. Light travels through the Ether (as light-waves) at the rate of 184,000 miles a second. The same is true of Heat and of Electricity. But Gravitation travels instantaneously. For instance, if a new star were to spring into existence at some inconceivable distance from the earth it would require thousands of years for its light to reach us. But its Attraction of Gravitation would be felt *instantly*. Do you realize what this means? It means that Gravitation is in some way connected with the Ether, or "conveying medium," that an impulse communicated at some point of space trillions of miles away is felt *at once* at our point in space, and vice versa. There is some awful mystery here, and the laws of Substance, and Force, as generally understood, do not account for it. And the theories regarding the Ether do not throw light upon it. *But wait a bit!*

But more than this. Science holds that Gravitation *does not require a medium*—that it seems to be its own medium—needing no "Ether" or other medium to transmit its influence. In this respect also, Gravitation differs from the form of Radiant Energy. And more, it is not "cut-off" or interfered with by any intervening body, for its force operates through such intervening bodies. For instance, in an eclipse of the Sun, the Moon passes between the Earth and the Sun, but the Gravitation is not affected in the slightest, for the bodies would evidence such change immediately were it to occur.

So Gravitation acts instantaneously; is its own medium, and may not be interfered with by an intervening body. It, indeed, is in a different "class" from Light, Heat and Electricity.

And now let us consider the other forms of Attraction.

In the previous chapters we saw that the form of Attraction called "Cohesion" caused the molecules to tend to each other, and to remain in more or less close contact, the differing degrees of Cohesion determining the Density, etc., of the body. Were the Attractive force of Cohesion suddenly removed, the most solid bodies, as well as the lightest ones, would instantly fly into very fine powder, thus being resolved into their constituent molecules. The separation of the Molecules, that is, the "setting further apart," occasioned by Heat, is spoken of by Physicists as "Repulsion." But the writer holds that repulsion is an entirely different thing, and that the heat merely causes the Molecules to lose a portion of their Attractive power for each other. Until the heat being withdrawn, the Molecules respond to the uninterrupted Attraction. The Molecules are like lovers who are attracted toward each other, and remain attached unless separated violently, or by some fading of Attraction. Consider Heat as a disturbing element—a "misunderstanding" between the molecular lovers, who under its influence draw somewhat apart, and are only reunited when the obstacle is removed, and harmony again manifested.

As we have shown you in a previous chapter, the so-called "properties" of Matter, *i.e.*, Hardness, Tenacity, Malleability, Ductility, etc., are simply evidence of a persistent Cohesiveness of the Molecules—a strong "love" or "desire" for each other that caused them to adopt every possible means in their power to resist, and prevent, the separation of the Molecules forming the mass. It was like a desperate attempt to prevent the "breaking up of the family."

Each so-called Special Physical Property of Matter is seen to be but the action of the Molecule resisting separation, in obedience to that law of its being called "Attraction," or "Gravitation," or "Cohesion," or "Adhesion"—but which might as fitly be called "Desire," or "Love." And, remember, that this law does not seem to be merely one of self-preservation of the Molecule—for it remains intact even after the separation from its companions or family. It is more, for it is a law that causes it to bend all its energies in remaining within "molecular distance" or close companionship with its family, and resisting disintegration. It is like the "social instinct" in Man, if one may be pardoned from using the figure.

Now for the Attraction of the Atoms—"Chemical Affinity," or "Chemism," as it is called. An Atom, you know, is the chemical unit of Matter, and the smallest particle of Matter that can enter into combination (leaving the Corpuscle out of the consideration, for the moment). These Atoms exhibit and manifest an Attraction for each other that causes them to form combinations or "marriages," and thus to combine, forming a molecule. But remember, always, that when Atoms "combine" they do not merge their identities—they simply "marry," and nothing more. Each atom maintains its own identity, and is found intact if the "marriage" is destroyed by chemical process, which might be called the termination of the molecular marriage, by "divorce," that is, by one Atom forsaking its mate and seeking a new "affinity" in the shape of some more attractive (or attracting) Atom. For, alas, the Atoms are more or less fickle, and often leave their life-partners for some other fascinating Particle. At times there is manifested a condition of "how happy could I be with either, were t'other fair charmer away"—there is a conflict of attractions.

There is more "flirting" and "affairs of the heart" in the world of Atoms than in the region of the Molecules, for while the latter are apt to seek only the companionship of their own "family," or some nearly related family, the Atoms have quite a number of possible "affinities," and will invariably desert a lesser attraction for a greater one (thus forming a new molecule) and leave the deserted one to get along alone as best it may, or else form a new alliance with some other affinity who is either impervious to the attraction of the more brilliant charmer, or else is out of the danger of temptation.

But, if we analyze and carefully consider this "Chemical Affinity," "Chemism," we will see that it comes well under the definition of "Attraction" as given by Webster, and quoted in the first part of this chapter. It certainly comes under the rule of "*the power in nature acting mutually between bodies, or ultimate particles, tending to draw them together*," etc.

The writer thinks that he is justified in asking you to consider Gravitation, Cohesion, Adhesion and Chemical Affinity as related forms of the same thing. If you do not like to call this "same thing" by the name of "Gravitation," suppose we call it "The Law of Attraction," of which Gravitation, Cohesion, Adhesion, Chemical Affinity or Chemism are but different aspects. (This "relation" is described in Chapter XIII.)

And the writer believes that this "Law of Attraction" is the underlying cause of all that we call Energy, Force, Power, Motion, etc., in the Physical world. For if "Gravitation" accounts for all "Mass Motion," or "Mechanical Motion"—if Molecular Cohesion, and the vibrations accompanying it, manifest in forms of "Molecular Motion"—and if Atomic "Chemical Affinity" or "Chemism," manifest in "Atomic Motion"—and if even the Corpuscles in their movements obey this same "Law of Attraction" in some form—and if all Force and Energy is but a "Mode of Motion"—then, if all this be true, are we not justified in claiming that this "Law of Attraction" is the Basis of All Energy, Force and Motion? And are we not justified in thinking of this "Law of Attraction" as always manifesting in the direction of drawing together particles of Substance—be those particles suns, planets, masses, molecules, atoms or corpuscles—in pursuance of some basic law imposed upon All-things, by That-which-is-above-Things?

The following quotation is interesting, in our consideration of this subject:

"There are other forces besides gravity, and one of the most active of these is chemical affinity. Thus, for instance, an atom of oxygen has a very strong attraction for one of carbon, and we may compare these two atoms to the earth and a stone lodged upon the top of a house. Within certain limits, this attraction is intensely powerful, so that when an atom of carbon and one of oxygen have been separated from each other, we have a species of energy of position just as truly as when a stone has been separated from the earth. Thus by having a large quantity of oxygen and a large quantity of carbon in separate states, we are in possession of a large store of *energy* of position. When we allowed the stone and the earth to rush together, the *energy* of position was transformed into that of actual motion, and we should therefore expect something similar to happen when the separated carbon and oxygen are allowed to rush together. This takes place when we burn coal in our fires, and the primary result, as far as *energy* is concerned, is the production of a large amount of heat. We are, therefore, led to conjecture that heat may denote a motion of particles on the small scale just as the rushing together of the stone and the earth denotes a motion on the large. It thus appears that we may have invisible molecular energy as well as visible mechanical *energy*."—*Balfour Stewart*.

To the writer it seems that the Particle of Substance finds within its Mind-principle (for you know we have seen that all Substance had something akin to Life and Mind) a constant craving, imbedded in its very nature, which causes it to seek Satisfaction. This craving for Satisfaction results in Unrest, and seeks a solution along two lines. These two lines are indicated by two entirely different Desires that it finds within itself—the first being a Desire or Inclination to seek the companionship of some other Particle—the second being a Desire or Inclination to be Free of Attachment or Entanglement.

The Desire for Attachment arises from the force of the Law of Attraction that exists between each Particle of Substance. The Desire for Non-attachment arises from some inward inclination for Freedom. These two Desires or Inclinations may be called the Desire for Impression and the Desire for Expression.

The Desire for Impression (or pressing in) manifests along lines of action tending toward Attachment, Moreness, Companionship, Combination. The Desire for Expression (or pressing out) manifests along the lines of action tending toward Individuality, Freedom, Independence, Unattachment, etc. And both are strong cravings—and both tend to produce Unrest, which results in Motion. The "pull" of the Desire of Impression exists always, and is always modified and counteracted by the "push" of the Desire for Expression. And, resulting from the play of these two Desires, or Forces, result Activity, Motion and Change. Like the two conflicting angels in the Persian mythology—Ahriman and Ormuzd—these two Desires wrestle with each other in the theatre of the Universe—constant Motion and Change being the results.

And, if the writer may be pardoned for dropping into Mysticism for the moment, may it not be that these conflicting Desires for Separateness and Unity, respectively, are but different forms of the Desire for Satisfaction through Oneness. Impression seeks Oneness by combination with other separated Particles, *but finds it not*. Expression seeks Oneness by drawing apart and endeavoring to realize it in that way, *but finds it not*. But both are but different aspects of the same Desire for Satisfaction, and only when the Mind recognizes Oneness in Diversity does Satisfaction come. And thus the lesson of the Particle becomes the Lesson of the Man.

These conflicting Desires of Inclinations of the Particles—the one urging it along the lines of Attraction—the other along the lines of Separation—produce the Dance of the Atoms—the Motion of the Particles.

When the Particle manifests along the lines of Expression it pushes itself away from the other Particle, and, consequently, also pushes the other Particle away. When it manifests along the lines of Impression, it pulls itself toward the other Particle, and at the same time pulls the other Particle toward itself. In both cases the "medium" of the pulling extends over the space separating them, as will be described in future chapters. This pulling and pushing is called by Chemistry "Attraction and Repulsion" of the Particles.

It is perhaps unnecessary to state that the Force of the Attraction of Cohesion or of Chemical Affinity is much stronger than that of Gravitation, in the case of the same Particles. Otherwise, if one picked up a piece of iron, the Attraction of Gravitation would cause its particles to separate and fall to the ground, whereas, the Attraction of Cohesion and that of Chemical Affinity enable the Particles to counteract the pull of Gravitation, and thus remain intact. Compared with Cohesion or Chemical Affinity, the pull of Gravitation is incomparably weak. The force which holds together two atoms of water represents a high degree of dynamic power, and the shock of forcible separation of chemical atoms produces something akin to an explosion. So we see that the Attraction of the Particles, while of the same nature as Gravitation, is much higher in intensity.

But notwithstanding the power of the Attraction, it seems to be a matter inherent in the nature of the Particle, and to represent a something like Will, in response to Desire.

The varying "push and pull" or the two Desires, would necessarily cause a revolution of each Particle on its own axis, and a revolution around each other—besides many instances of rushing together and away from each other. In these forms of Motion is to be found the cause of the vibrations producing Radiant Energy, known as Light, Heat, Electricity and Magnetism.

CHAPTER-XI
The Theory of Dynamic Thought

FROM the preceding chapters we have learned that:

(1) The forms of Force or Radiant Energy, known as Light, Heat, Magnetism and Electricity, are "Modes of Motion," arising from the Original Motion of the Particles of Substance (Molecules, Atoms, Corpuscles or Electrons). And that such Original Motion of the Particles arises from the Operation of The Law of Attraction;

(2) That the forms of Attractive Force or Energy, known as Gravitation, Cohesion, Adhesion, Atomic Attraction, Chemical Affinity or Chemism, and Corpuscular Attraction, also arise from the operation of the Law of Attraction;

(3) That, from the above, it follows that: All Manifestations of Force and Energy in Inorganic Substance (*viz.*, both Radiant Energy in its forms of Light, Heat, Magnetism, Electricity, etc.; and also Attractive Energy in its forms of Gravitation, Cohesion, Adhesion, Chemical Affinity or Atomic Attraction and Corpuscular Attraction) arise from the operation of the Law of Attraction.

It will be well to remember that the fact that some of the above forms of Radiant Force or Energy, such as Heat, Light, Magnetism and Electricity, may arise from Motion transmitted from other Substance, does not alter the matter. For if they arise from "waves" from some other Substance, it merely follows that the Original Motion that gave rise to the "waves" arose from the operation of the Law of Attraction. Or, if they arise from "interrupted Motion," it merely follows that the Motion that is interrupted may be traced back to Original Motion that arose from the operation of the Law of Attraction. So that all Mechanical Power, and all the forms of Energy or Force producing the same (omitting for the moment the forms of Energy or Force of "Living Organisms," which will be described later on) arise from the operation of the Law of Attraction.

Now, for the next step. We have seen that the operation of the Law of Attraction results from Vital-Mental Action on the part of the Life and Mind Principle inherent in the nature of the Particles of Substance. Consequently, all forms of Energy and Force arising from the operation of The Law of Attraction—the latter being the result of Vital-Mental Action—then it follows that:

All forms of Energy and Force having its origin in the Law of Attraction are manifestations of Vital-Mental Action.

But this is not all—for we have not considered the Energy and Force abiding in, and manifested by, what are called "Living Organisms," such as human, animal and plant life, which are manifested by the physical organisms or "bodies" of man, animal and plant. In order to avoid a long digression into the realms of biology, we will omit all but a passing reference to the theories that seek to identify the action of the cells of organic life with those of the particles of inorganic life—for remember, that Organic Substance has its Molecules, Atoms and Corpuscles, as well as its higher combinations known as "Cells"—and we will seek the ultimate source of all forms of Force and Energy, exhibited by "Organic Life," in that which lies back of "Physical Action." We need no argument here—for all will readily recognize that behind the physical action of man, animal and plant, lies Life and Mind, and that therefore all Force and Energy arising from such action must be manifestations of Vital-Mental Action.

And so, summing up our conclusions regarding Force and Energy and Motion in Inorganic Substance—and then in Organic Substance—we arrive at an understanding of the Basic Proposition of the Theory of Dynamic Thought, which is as follows:

Basic Proposition.—*That All forms and exhibition of Force, Energy, Motion and Power are manifestations of Vital-Mental Action. And that, consequently, at the last there is no Force but Vital-Mental Force; no Energy but Vital-Mental Energy; no Motion but Vital-Mental Motion; no Power but Vital-Mental Power.*

It is possible that the average reader will fail to recognize the tremendous importance of the above proposition. It is most revolutionary, and is not only directly opposed to the Materialistic theory which makes Matter the dominant factor—the only factor, in fact—in Life; but it is also far different from the opinion of the average person who has been taught to think of "blind force," "dead matter," "mechanical energy," "power of machinery, engines," etc. And yet, you are invited to go back over the path that leads up to the theory, and test and examine every bit of the road for weak spots—insecure bridges, etc.—the writer feels that the work will bear examination. He thinks that he has succeeded not only in proving that (1) The Universe is Alive and Thinking; and (2) That Mind is Dominant—but he believes, also, that he has made at least partially understandable the old occult and metaphysical aphorism that has been heard so much in these later days—the statement that "All is Mind—Mind is All."

The only fact needed now is the proof of the old occult theory that Matter or Substance blends gradually into Mind, and that in the end it is found to have its origin there. So far, Science has not given us this proof, but it begins to look that way, although Science does not dream of what lies at the end of the road she is travelling. She tells us that she sees Matter melting into Force or Energy, and that perhaps the Universe may be found to be Energy or Force, at the last. But she ignores the fact that her investigations have already proven (to those who know how to combine them) that Mind is back of Force—that all Force is Mental Force, at the last. And, so, you see it is not so far a cry from Matter to Mind in these days of the Twentieth Century. The bridge is being erected by the Materialists, but the Mentalist will be the first to cross over it.

But there are many important questions ahead of us for consideration in relation to the Theory of Dynamic Thought. And we must hasten on to them.

One of the first questions that must be considered is that of the transmission of Force, Energy or Motion. Science has told us that Light travels and is "contagious," that Heat travels and is "contagious," that Electricity travels and is "contagious," that Magnetism travels and is "contagious." But is has failed to find evidences of Cohesive Force, or Adhesive Force, or the Force of Gravitation, or the Force of Chemical Affinity, or the Force of Corpuscular Affinity, being "contagious," and although it recognizes that they must "travel" beyond the limits of the bodies manifesting them, yet it has hazarded no theory or hypothesis, worthy of the name, to account for the phenomenon. It informs us that Light, Heat, Magnetism and Electricity "travel" (via waves of the "Ether") at the rate of 184,000 miles per second—and that when they reach their destination the "Ether waves" set up similar vibrations in the Substance with which they come in contact. The only explanation of the method or medium of "travel" is the "Aristotle's Ether" Theory, which, while generally accepted as a working hypothesis, nevertheless, brings a broad smile to the face of any thoughtful scientist who considers it in detail. As for the medium of the transmission of Gravitation, Cohesion, Chemical Affinity and Molecular Affinity, Science is mute. All that she says is that Gravitation is believed to travel *instantaneously* over distances that it takes Light, travelling at the rate of 184,000 miles per second, *over two thousand years* to travel. Verily, Gravitation defies Scientific theories and estimates, and laughs at the "Ether." Let us see if the Dynamic Thought Theory throws any light on the subject!

The first step in the solution of the problem of the transferring and communication of Energy is the remembrance of the fact that the Energy is *purely Mental*. Be it Gravitation, Affinity or Attraction, on the one hand—or Light, Heat, Magnetism or Electricity on the other—it is all Mental Force. Attraction in all of its forms has been recognized as Mental Action. And the vibrations that cause Light, Heat, Magnetism and Electricity have been seen to result from the Law of Attraction, and, therefore, are Mental. This being the case, would it not be wise for us to look for a solution of the transmission of Force and Energy in the region from which it originated—*the Mental Region*? Does not this seem reasonable? Should not the explanation for Mental Effects be sought in a Mental Cause? And should not the medium between Mind and Mind be looked for in the Mental Region?

Taking the liberty of peeping into some of the succeeding chapters of this book—getting a little ahead of the story, as it were—let us consider the operation of Mind in the higher forms of Life. Without argument, or proof at this point, let us remember the well-founded statements of fact—and the old occult teachings as well—that the Mind is not confined to the limits of the body, but extends as an "Aura" for some distance beyond the physical form. Let us also remember the phenomena grouped together under the general subject of "Thought-transference," "Thought-transmission," "Telepathy," or (the best term of all) "Telesthesia" (meaning, literally "far-off sensation"). The writer imagines that he hears the yell of derision go up at this point from the materialistic personage, or "man on the street," who has been induced to read this book by some well meaning friend. "Thought-transference, Fiddlesticks," we may hear him cry, in imagination. But let this reader remember—Fiddlesticks, or no Fiddlesticks—that Thought-transmission is a proven fact—and that thousands of people *know* it to be so, absolutely, from their own experience. It is too late in the day for sneers at the mention of the term.

Well, then, since Force is Mental, and we are looking for a Mental explanation for the phenomenon of Transmission of Force, does it not seem natural to consider Thought-transmission in that connection? Answering a possible objection of some critical reader, to the effect that before a "sensation" may be received, the receiver must have "sense-organs"—a very good objection, but one that is answered by Science itself—let us read on.

Haeckel, the distinguished scientist, in his endeavor to prove that Man's senses are but a development of something in inorganic life, has called our attention to the fact that Molecules, and Atoms, are capable of "receiving" sensations and "responding" thereto. He makes quite a point of this in his latest works, and remarks, among many other things showing his positive views on the subject of "sensation in the inorganic world": *"I cannot imagine the simplest chemical and physical process without attributing the movements of the material particles to unconscious sensation";* and again: *"The idea of chemical affinity consists in the fact that the various chemical elements perceive the qualitative differences in other elements—experience 'pleasure' or 'revulsion' at contact with them, and execute specific movements on this ground."* He also quotes, approvingly, the remarks of Nageli, who said: *"If the molecules possess something that is related, however distantly, to sensation, it must be comfortable to be able to follow their attractions and repulsions; uncomfortable when they are forced to do otherwise."* Haeckel also says that in his opinion *the sensations in animal and plant life are "connected by a long series of evolutionary stages with the simpler forms of sensation that we find in the inorganic elements, and that reveal themselves in chemical affinity."* Is not this strong enough? Perhaps we may now be permitted at least to "assume" that even the Atoms, Molecules and Corpuscles have "something like sensation."

Some one may now object that Haeckel speaks of "contact" between the particles, and that sensation by contact (even in an atom) is far different from sensation without contact, at a short distance. Quite right, but if the objector will take the trouble to review the teachings of Science regarding the relation of the Particles, he will see that the Particles are *never "exactly" in contact*, except in moments of collision, which, by the way, they carefully avoid. The Corpuscles, as we have shown, have *"plenty of room" in which to move about*, and they move in orbits around each other. The Atoms combine, *but there is always room between them*, as may be seen by reference to the teachings regarding the "Ether," which "fills up the cracks" according to the theory. And the Molecules *also have "plenty of room,"* as may be seen by reference to that part of the subject, particularly to the comparison of the drop of water magnified to the size of the Earth, in which the Molecules would appear about the size of the original drop *with more room between each than their own size*.

In fact, as we have been shown in a previous chapter, the particles are attracted only to a certain distance, at which they resist the impulse or attraction and "stand off" a bit. They will not be forced too near without creating disturbances, and manifestations of force, and if they are separate beyond a certain distance the attractive power ceases to operate. But *there is always some room between them*, and they bridge over that room and exert and receive the attractive power *in some way*. This is true not only of the particles but of the great bodies, like the Earth and planets, that are attracted, and attract over great distances. Now for the question: "How do they exert sense and attractive power over the great comparative distance—great, comparatively, as well in atom, as in planet and sun?"

Some one may answer the question closing the last paragraph with the word "*Electricity*." Very good—Electricity, like the "Ether," comes in quite handy when one is forced to explain something not known. "Electricity," like the "Glacial Period," "Aristotle's Ether," "Natural Laws," and "Suggestion," is a most handy weapon of argument, and often acts as a preventative to further inquiry and investigation until some sufficiently irreverent of precedent arises to ask, "But Why and How?" and starts the ball rolling again.

But "Electricity" will not answer in this case, for the rate of the "travel" of Electricity is well known—184,000 miles per second, which, fast as it is, assumes the crawl of a "slow-freight" when compared with the "instantaneous" rate of travel of Gravitation. And then Electricity requires a "medium" and Gravitation does not, and in many other ways the two are seen to be totally different. And in the case of the Space between the Atom and Molecule and Corpuscle, it is no more reasonable to say "Electricity" than it would be to say "Heat" or "Light"; and "Magnetism" is not available for obvious reasons. Remember that Electricity, Light and Heat are *caused* by Motion resulting from Attraction, and *the child cannot procreate the parent*. Heat, Light and Electricity may beget each other (and they do). And Gravitation may procreate Heat, Light and Electricity. But Heat, Light and Electricity *cannot procreate Gravitation*—Never! And Light, Heat and Electricity require replenishing from the common source of Energy, but Gravitation is self-sufficient and asks no replenishing or storage-battery or power-house. Electricity, Heat and Light come and go, appearing, manifesting and disappearing, swallowed up by each other, or by Substance. But Gravitation is always there—unchangeable—unwavering—immutable—invariable—Something above Matter and Force—something majestic, awe-inspiring, sublime! Does it take a wild flight of the imagination to see that this Something, that is not Matter, and nor Force, *must be a manifestation of Mind*?

Let us first apply this idea of Thought-transference to the operation of the Law of Attraction between the Corpuscles, Atoms and Molecules of Substance—the Particles of Substance. The particles are believed to move to or away from each other in accordance with the workings of Attraction and Affinity, in its various degrees. First they must *desire* to move—not Desire in the developed sense that we feel it, but still elementary "feeling," or "inclination," or "tendency"—call it what you will, but it remains rudimentary Mental Emotion—an E-motion leading to Motion. (This is not a pun—look up the meaning of the word Emotion and you will see its application.)

Then, following the Desire, comes the action in the direction of gratifying it. The Particles act to gratify Desire in two ways—acting at a "distance," remember—they exert the Attractive Force, which the writer believes to be Mental Force, *transmitted by Mind, projection*, a mental or psychic bond or connection being thus established. By means of this bond of Mind, the Particle endeavors to (1) draw itself to the object; and (2) to draw the object toward itself. In the case of the Molecule, this Desire and Movement seems to be mutual, and evidenced by and to all Molecules alike, *providing they be within Molecular Distance*, as Science calls it. But in the case of the Atoms, it seems to be different—for there is found a greater degree of "choice," or "elective affinity." This "election" or "choice" is not altogether free, but depends upon the relative likes and dislikes of certain "kinds" of elements, as we have seen in previous chapters, although, to be sure, these Elements are all made out of the same "stuff" in different combinations.

The details of Corpuscular Attraction are not known, so it cannot be told whether "preferences" exist, or whether (in the words of the street) all Corpuscles "look alike" to each other. It would appear, however, that there must be some reasons for preference, among the Corpuscles, else they would always form in the same combinations—always act alike to each other, as they are alike in other actions—and thus there would be but *one* Element or kind of Atom, formed, instead of the *seventy-five*, already known. To be sure, in this case, it *might* be that the *one* kind of Atom formed would be the Atom of Hydrogen, and that all other Elements, or Atoms, were modifications of that one—just proving the dream of the Scientists of the Nineteenth Century. But, as Kipling would say, "that is another story."

To return to the Particle which we left trying to draw the other Particle to itself, and itself toward the other. There is no *material* connection between them (and Electricity and Magnetism will not answer), so what is to be done? Evidently the Particle knows, for it exerts *a "drawing" power or force by means of the Mental-connection*, and two come together. The Particle evidently is able to exert a repelling or "moving away" power by reversing the process, the Mental-bond acting as the medium. This may cause a smile, because we have never seen an instance of bodies pulling themselves together by intangible "bonds." *Haven't we?* Then how about two pieces of magnetised steel, or two electrified substances? Oh, that's different, you say. *Why, different?* Isn't *the bond intangible*? And, haven't we seen that both Electricity and Magnetism were Mental Actions also? Oh,—er—but well,—oh yes, *that's* it—perhaps the Attracting Force is Magnetism or Electricity. No, that will not do, for we have seen that Electricity and Magnetism were *products* of this Attraction, not *producers* of it—the Attraction must come *before* Electricity and Magnetism, not *after* them—you are mixing Cause and Effect. And, even if you were right—and you cannot be—wouldn't the Electrical or Magnetic Force be *called into operation, and directed by the Mental Action*, arising from the Desire? You cannot get away from Mental Action when you study the Law of Attraction.

"But, how about the fact that Heat causes the Particles to change their vibrations, and draw apart, and all that sort of thing—and Electricity, likewise?" you may ask. "Surely this takes the matter away from Mental Action, doesn't it?" Well, the writer thinks that the phenomenon referred to only helps to prove his theory. And he will endeavor to so prove to you.

The consideration of the facts related in this chapter, leads us to a supplemental proposition to our Basic Proposition, which may be stated as follows:

SUPPLEMENTAL PROPOSITION I.—*Not only is the Law of Attraction the manifestation of a Mental Process, or Vital-Mental Action; but also the actual Force or Energy used in bringing the Particles of Substance in closer relation, in accordance with that Law, is in its nature a Vital Mental Force or Energy, operating between bodies or particles of Substance, without a material medium.*

CHAPTER-XII

The Law of Vibrant Energy

IN previous chapters we have seen that the phenomena of Radiant Energy, known as Light, Heat, Magnetism and Electricity, had their origin in the Motion of the Particles, the different classes of phenomena depending upon the particular degree and nature of the aforesaid Motion of Particles.

We have seen also that Radiant Energy could be communicated or transmitted from one body of Substance to another. And that the communication of transmission might be accomplished not only by close contact of the bodies, but by "waves" of some sort which were caused in some "medium" (the Ether) by the vibrations of the Particles of the body, and which "waves," when they reached the other body, were transformed into vibrations of the Particles corresponding to those manifested in the first body. The idea has been illustrated by the sending telephone, the sound waves in the diaphragm of which were transformed into waves of the Electric current, and thus passing along the wires were transformed again into sound-waves by the diaphragm of the receiving instrument.

We have seen, also in the preceding chapter, that the medium by which these vibrations were transferred, transmitted, or communicated, might be supposed to be Mind, the operation being akin to Thought-transference. Now let us examine into the workings of the matter.

In the first place, we assume a certain state of vibration, existing in a certain body of Substance—Heat, or Electricity for instance (either illustration will answer.) Another body of Substance is brought in close contact with the first body, and the vibrations of Energy pass on to the second, not by "waves" but by a seeming actual passing of vibrations without the need of intervening "waves." This, Science calls transmission by Conduction, the theory being that the particles rapidly "pass on" the vibrations from one to another. Convection or conduction along other forms of Substance, such as hot-air, hot-water-steam, etc., is but a variation of the above, as Substance is the medium in both cases. The third form of transmission is by Radiation, whereby the vibrations are transmitted by "waves" in some medium other than Substance (according to the theory), as we have described in a preceding paragraph, as well as in previous chapters. As a matter of fact, a careful analysis of the matter will show that even in the "Conduction" of the most solid Substance, there must be a "*medium not Substance*" between the Particles of the Substance, *for the Particles always have Space between them*—this being true of the Particles of Air, as well as those of Iron. *So there is always Space to be traversed by a "medium not Substance."* But we need not stop to split-hairs regarding this question, for the general explanation will explain this also.

Now, to get back to our body of Substance vibrating with Radiant Energy, separated from a second body of Substance by a great distance—thousands of miles in fact—millions would be better—let us take two worlds, for instance—the Sun and the Earth. Ignoring for the moment the explanation of Gravitations (which will be given later) and realizing that there *is no medium of Substance* existing between the two bodies, we must grant that there is a "*medium not Substance*" existing between them, either permanently or thrown out for the purpose of this special transmission. We shall assume a medium existing before the need of the transmission (for reasons to be seen later.) Our Theory of Dynamic Thought, and Thought-Transference between bodies of Substance, compels us to suppose that this medium *is a Mental Connection, or Mental Relation, existing between the two bodies of Substance*. So, we must consider the question of this medium of Mind transmitting the vibrations of Radiant Energy from the Sun to the Earth. How can Mind conduct Radiant Energy? *It does not conduct Radiant Energy*, but it does *transmit*—not Radiant Energy—but the *Mental State that causes Radiant Energy Vibrations*.

This statement of a "Mental State causing Radiant Energy Vibrations" seems rather startling at first sight—but let us examine it. We have seen that the Radiant Energy was caused by the Motion or Vibrations of the Particles, which Motion or Vibration was the result of the workings of the Law of Attraction, and which Law was but the manifestation of Vital-Mental Action. And, at the last, the Vibrations of Radiant Energy are the result of peculiar or particular "states" of the Life and Mind of the Particle. The word "State" is derived from the Latin word *Status*, meaning "position; standing," and is used generally in the sense of "condition."

This Mental State of the Particle may be described as a state of "*Emotional Excitement*." Let us pause a moment to consider the meaning of these words—it often helps us to understand a subject, if we examine the real meaning of the words defining it. "Emotion" is derived from the Latin word *Emotum*, meaning "to shake; to stir up"—the Latin word being made up of two other words, *i.e.*, *E*, meaning "out"; and Motum, "to move." "Emotion" is defined as "a moving or excitement of the mind." "Excitement" is derived from the Latin word *Excitare*, meaning "to move out"—the English word being defined as "a calling to Activity; state of Active feeling; aroused Activity." So you see that the idea of *Active Motion*, and *Aroused Activity*, of Mind, permeates the term "Emotional Excitement," that is used by the writer in connection with the Mental State causing vibration of the Particles of Substance. The single word, "Excitement," will be used by the writer, hereafter, in the above connection, in order to avoid complex terms. To those who still object to the use of a mental term in reference to motion of Substance, he might remark that Science makes use of the term—"Excite," and "Excitement"—in reference to Electrical phenomena, so that he is not altogether without support in the use of the word.

Now to return again to our body of Substance—the Sun—the Particles of which are manifesting a great degree of "Excitement," evidencing in Vibrations producing the phenomenon of Radiant Energy. The excitement is shared equally by its Particles, the "contagion" having spread among them. Even the Particles of its atmosphere are vibrating with Excitement, and evidencing Radiant Energy. The Sun is in direct Mental Connection with the Earth (as we shall see presently) and the Excitement is transmitted by Thought-Transference (along this Mental Connection) in the shape of Dynamic Thought-waves of Excitement. These waves have a rate of speed of 184,000 miles per second—why this particular rate, or any rate at all, is not apparent; it being very evident, however, that this particular kind of Mental Action—Excitement, or Thought—is not transmitted *instantaneously* as is the Mental Quality known as Desire, resulting in Attraction, or Gravitation, which seems to be rather a Basic quality, rather than a temporary disturbance or emotional excitement. But the writer must not get ahead of his story.

The Excitement of the Particles of Substance composing the Sun is "contagious," and the Thought-waves travel along the Mental Connection, or medium, at a wonderful rate of speed. Soon they come in contact with the Mental Atmosphere of the Earth and the Excitement becomes manifest in Action, the Emotional Excitement being reproduced by the Particles of the Earth's Substance nearest the surface which vibrate and manifest the Radiant Energy in spite of themselves, for the tendency among Particles is to "settle down," and remain "calm," rather than to participate in Emotional Excitement. They have acquired a normal and fixed rate of Vibration, or Mental State, after many years, gradually changing from a high state of Excitement, to a comparative calm state. And, their tendency and inclination is Conservative, and they are disposed to resent and repel Radical states of Excitement or Disturbance, coming from other less Conservative Bodies.

The above fact partially explains why the communicated Excitement manifests itself more strongly on the surface of the body "exposed" to the contagion of Excitement. The Conservative influence is always at work, and manages to absorb and equally distribute the Energy that is beating down upon it, without allowing it to penetrate very far. The Energy is used-up or absorbed, and neutralized by the lower vibrations of the Mass. The effort of the Energy coming from the sending Body is to "bring-up" the vibrations of the receiving body to the rate of the sender; while the effort of the receiving body is to resist this effort, and to reduce and "bring-down" the transmitted increased rate of vibration of the Particles immediately exposed to the contagion. In both cases the effort is toward "equalization" of the rate of vibrations. This working of the law may be observed plainly in the case of Heat vibrations—the Energy seeming to wish to "bring-up" the vibrations or temperature of the second body, while the latter resists this effort, and strives to "bring-down" the vibrations or temperature of those Particles of itself that have "caught the Motion." The Energy is like a Radical Agitator who wishes to stir up an Excitement, leading to "a change," while the Body is like the Conservative element that prefers to "let well enough alone," and resists the stirring-up process, and exerts itself to restore quiet, and to maintain accustomed conditions.

The explanation of the phenomenon given in any work on Physics or Natural Philosophy will answer fairly well in the consideration of this Theory of Dynamic Thought, the only important change being required, being the substitution of "Thought-waves" for "Waves of the Ether" of Science. Science has described the "working operations," as might be expected from her years of careful study and examination. She has erred only in the Theory or Hypothesis advanced to account for the facts. Her "Ether" handed down by Aristotle, is admitted by her to be paradoxical and "unthinkable"—but she has had none other to substitute for it. She will probably sneer at the Dynamic Thought, and Thought-Transference theory advanced in this book—if indeed she takes the trouble to examine it. But sometime, from her own ranks—among her most advanced members—will arise a man who will claim that "All Force is Mental Force," and that

"Transference of Energy is Thought Transference." And the Scientific World will accept the doctrine after it finds itself unable to fight it down—and it will give new names and terms to its workings. And it will proclaim loudly the "new" Truth. And this little book, and its writer will be ignored—but its work will go on. The writer although probably doomed to have himself and his theory laughed at by the masses of people (whose children will accept the teachings of this book) does not feel discouraged by the prospect. He cares nothing for personal credit—the truth being the important thing. Like Galvini, (whose words appear on the title page of this book) he may cry: *"I am attacked by two very opposite sects—the scientists and the know-nothings. Both laugh at me, calling me the 'Frog's Dancing Master,' but I know that I have discovered one of the greatest Forces in Nature."* The illustration given above of the transmission of the Excitement of the Particles of the Sun to the Particles of the Earth, will answer equally well in the case of Light, Heat, Magnetism and Electricity. And it will answer in the case of the transmission of these Forces between Atoms, Molecules, and Masses as well as between Worlds and Solar Systems. Any bodies subject to the Law of Attraction may and do, so transmit Vibrations. In our consideration of "The Riddle of the Sphinx," which forms the subject of the next chapter, we shall obtain further particulars of the workings of the Law.

The consideration of the facts and principles stated in this chapter brings us to a second Supplemental Proposition, which may be stated as follows:

SUPPLEMENTAL PROPOSITION II.—*The rates of vibration of the Particles of Substance may be likened to "Mental States"; and a high degree of the same may be called an "Excitement." This "Excitement" may be, and is, communicated from the Particles of the body manifesting it, to the Particles of other bodies—the medium of such communication being a Mental Connection or Mental Relation existing between the two bodies of Substance, without the employment of any material medium—and which Excitement, so communicated, reproduces in the second body the vibrations manifested in the first body, subject, always, to the counteracting efforts of the second body to maintain its accustomed, and former, rate of vibration, and Mental State.*

CHAPTER-XIII

The Riddle of The Sphinx

IT is with no light emotion, or jaunty air, that the writer approaches this part of his subject. On the contrary, he feels something like awe when he contemplates the nature of that great Something which he is called upon to attempt to "explain" in a few pages. He feels, in only a lighter degree, the emotion that one experiences when, in occasional moments, his mind leads to a contemplation of The Infinite. He feels that that which men mean when they say "Gravitation" and "The Ether," are but symbols and feeble concepts of Something so far above human experience that the Mind of Man may grasp only its lowest shadings, the greater and higher part of it, like the higher rays of the Spectrum, being hidden from the experience of Man.

In his endeavor to pass on to you his ideas regarding the Something that explains both Gravitation and the Ether, he must ask you to endeavor to form a Mental Picture of a "Something." This Something must fill all Space within the Limits of the Universe, or Cosmos—if limits it has. It must be an expression of the first of the attributes of The Infinite—the one called Omnipresence, or Presence-everywhere—and *yet it must not be The Infinite Presence*. It also must be an expression of the second of the attributes of the Infinite—the one called Omnipotence, or All-Power—and *yet it must not be The Infinite Power*. It also must be an expression of the third attribute of The Infinite—the one called Omniscience, or All-Knowing—and *yet it must not be The Infinite Wisdom*. It must be an expression of All the Attributes that *we think of* as belonging to The Infinite—*and yet through them All we may see The Infinite, Itself, in the background, viewing its expressions*.

This Something that you are asked to think of is that Something regarding which the mystics have dreamed; the philosophers have speculated; the scientists have sneered and smiled—that Something that Men have thought of as The Universal Mind or the Cosmic Mind.

You are asked to think of this Something as a great Ocean of Pure Mind, permeating all Space—between Solar Systems—between Worlds—between

Masses of Substance—between the Molecules, Atoms, and Corpuscles. In and about and around everything—yes, even in Everything—in the very essence of the Corpuscle it is—in truth *it is that Essence itself.*

Bound up in the bosom of that Mighty Ocean of Mind must reside all Knowledge of the Universe—of all "this side of God." For that All-Knowledge is but a knowing of its own region. Latent within itself must be locked up all Energy, or capacity for Force or Motion, for all Force or Energy is Mental. In its very presence it exemplifies the capacity of filling All Space. Omnipresent; Omnipotent; Omniscient—all the attributes of The Infinite are manifested in it—*and yet it is but the outward expression of That-Behind-the-Veil, which is the Causeless Cause of All.*

In that Great Ocean of Universal or Cosmic Mind, bodies of Substance are but as floating specks of dust—*or even bubbles formed of the substance of that Ocean itself*—on the surface of that Ocean, there may arise waves, currents, ripples, eddies, whirlpools,—storms, hurricanes, tempests,—from its bosom may rise vapor, that after stages of clouds, rain-drops, flowing in streams, rivers, bays, at last again reach the source of its origin. These disturbances and changes we call Energy, Force, Motion—but they are but surface manifestations, and the Great Ocean is serene in its depths, and, in reality, is unchanged and undisturbed.

This, friends, is that which the writer asks you to accept in the place of Aristotle's Ether. Is it a worthy exchange?

We have seen that the Attraction of Gravitation was different from any other so-called form of Force and Energy—both in its operations and laws, as well as in its constancy and self-support. And that it was different from the other forms of Attraction such as Cohesion, Chemical Affinity, etc. And, so we must consider it as more than a mere "Emotional Excitement" in the Mind of the Particle—that bubble on the surface of the Ocean. And it must be different from the special forms of Attraction manifested by the Atom and Molecule. It must be a simpler, more basic, and yet a more constant and permanent thing. It must exist before and after "Excitement; Vibration; Cohesion; and Chemical Affinity." *It must be the Mother of the Forces.*

Let us imagine the Cosmic Mind as a great body of Something filling Space, instead of as the surface of the Ocean, which figure we used just now—either figure is equally correct. This great Cosmic Mind is to be thought of as filling Space, and containing within its volume (Oh, for a better word!) countless worlds, and suns, as well as smaller bodies of Substance. These suns and world, and bodies are apparently free and unconnected, floating in this great volume of Mind. But they are not free and unconnected—they are linked together by a web of lines of Gravitation. Each body of Substance has a line reaching out in a continuous direction, and connecting it with another body. Each body has one of such lines connecting it with *each* particular "other body." Consequently, each body has countless lines reaching out from it; some slender, and some thick,—the thickness depending upon the ratio of distances maintained by, and relative sizes of, the particular bodies that it connects. This system of "lines" form a great net-work of connections in the volume of Mind, crossing each other at countless points (but not interfering with each other.) And although the number may be said to be "countless," still these lines do not begin to cover the entire dimensions of Space, or of the Mind that fills it. There are great areas of Space entirely untouched by these lines. If one could see the system of lines, it probably would appear as a sheared off section of a great spider's web, with lines in all directions, but with "plenty of room" between the lines. *Perhaps these lines converge to a common centre, and that centre may be——!* But this is transcendental dreaming—let us proceed with our consideration of the use of these lines.

It is to be understood, of course, that these "lines" *are not material* lines—not made of Substance—but rather, "conditions" in the Cosmic Mind. Not Thought-waves arising from the Excitement of Particles, but Something more basic, simpler, and more permanent. Let us look closer and we will see that the great lines of Gravitation radiating from, and connecting world with world—sun with planet—are really cables composed of much smaller lines, the finest strands of which are seen to emanate from each Corpuscle or Particle of Substance—the "line" of Gravitation reaching from the Earth to the Sun being composed of a mass of tiny strands which connect each Particle of one body with each Particle of the other. The last analysis shows us that *each Particle is connected with every other Particle in the Universe by a line of Attraction.*

These "Lines of Attraction" are what we call Gravitation—purely Mental in nature—Lines of Mind-Principle in the great volume of mind.

These lines of Gravitation must have existed from the creation of the Particle, and the connection between Particle and Particles must have existed from the beginning, if beginning there was. The Particles may have changed their positions and relations in the Universe, but the lines have never been broken. Whether the Particle existed as a free Corpuscle—whether combined as Atom or Molecule—whether part of this world or sun or planet, or that one countless millions of miles removed—it mattered not. The Line of Gravitation always was there, between that Particle and every other Particle. Distance extended and thinned the line, or the reverse, as the case might be—but it was there, always. Obstacles proved no hindrance to passage, for the lines passed through the obstacle. Can it not be seen that here is the secret of the fact that no "time" is required for the passage of Gravitation—it apparently traveling instantaneously, whereas, in fact, it does not "travel" at all. And does not seem that this theory also explains why no medium is required for the "travel" of Gravitation? And does it not explain why Gravitation is not affected in its "passage" by intervening bodies? Gravitation does not "travel" or "pass"—it remains constant, and ever present between the articles, varying in degree as the distance between the Particles is increased, and *vice-versa*; and increasing and decreasing in effect, according to the number of Particles combining their lines of Attraction, as in the case of Atom, Molecule, Mass, World. Gravitation is a Mental Connection or Bond uniting the Mind in the several Particles, rather than their Substance or Material.

Along these lines of Gravitation pass the "Thought-waves," resulting from the Excitement of the Particles—these fleeting, changing, inconstant waves of Emotion—how different they are from the changeless, constant exhibition of Gravitation. And along these same lines—when shortened by close contact, travel the impulses of Cohesion and Chemical Affinity. Gravitation not only performs its own work, but also acts as a "common-carrier" for the waves of Desire-Force, and the Thought-waves of Excitement of the Particles, manifesting as Attractive Energy, and Radiant Energy, respectively.

The writer asks you to remember, particularly, that while the Desire-waves of the Particles,—and their Thought-waves of Excitement—are changeable, disconnected, and inconstant; the Line of Gravitation is never broken, and could not be unless the Particle of Substance was swept out of existence, in which case the balance of the Universe would be overturned, and chaos would result. The Divine Plan is perfect to the finest detail—every Particle is needed—is known—is counted—and used in the Plan. And Gravitation is the plainest evidence of the REALITY of The Infinite that is afforded us. *In it we see the actual machinery of The Infinite.* No wonder that great thinkers have bowed their heads reverently before its Power and Awfulness, when their minds have finally grasped its import. Verily the sparrow's fall is noted, and known, as the Biblical writer has recorded, for the fall is in obedience to that great Law that holds the Particles in their places—that makes possible the whirl of worlds, and the existence of Solar Systems—that, indeed, makes possible the Forms of Life as we know them—that Something that forever and ever has, and will, silently, ceaselessly, untiringly, and without emotion, fulfilled its work and destiny—GRAVITATION.

The Theory of Dynamic Thought also holds that in addition to the existence of the Cosmic Mind, or Ocean of Mind-principle—and the Lines of Attraction that run through it, each particle has its Mental Atmosphere, or Aura. The Aura is an Atmosphere of Mind that surrounds the Particle—and also the larger bodies—and also living forms higher in the scale. This Aura is merely an extension of the bit of Mind that is segregated or apparently separated from the Cosmic Mind, for use by the individual Particle, Mass, or Creature. Through, and by means of this Aura the Particle takes cognizance of the approach and nature of the other Particles in its vicinity. The same rule holds good in the case of the Creatures, including Man, as we shall see in a later chapter. The fact is mentioned here, merely in order to connect the several manifestation of Mental Phenomena mentioned in the several parts of this book.

Some may object to the Theory of the Lines of Gravitation being the only "carriers" of the Energy of the Sun, as being contrary to the conception of Science that the Sun radiates Energy *in all directions equally*, just as does a piece of hot iron, or a lamp. Answering this objection, the writer would say that there is a decided difference in the two cases. The iron or lamp radiates its heat and light to the particles of the surrounding air and other Substance in close distance, the "lines" being very close together,—so close in fact that they seem to be continuous and having no space between them, at least no Space sufficiently large to be detected by the eye of Man, or his instruments. But with the Sun the case is different, for the distances are greater and the lines spread apart as the distance is increased. Draw a diagram of many fine rays emanating from a central point, and you will have the idea at once. If Space were filled with Substance, just as is the Atmosphere of the Earth—the Air, is meant of course—then indeed would the lines practically be joined together, but as Space between the worlds is almost devoid of Substance, the lines between the Sun and the other worlds, and planets, spread out rapidly as the distance from the Sun increases.

To show how this objection is really an additional proof of the Theory the writer begs to call your attention to the fact that according to the calculations of the physicists in Science, the Sun's energy would have been exhausted in 20,000,000 years, granting that it was dispersed equally in all directions during that time. But, *note this*, Science in its other branches, namely in Geology, etc., holds that the Sun already has been throwing out energy for 500,000,000 or more years, and seems able to stand the strain for many millions of years more. Thus Science is arrayed against Science. Does not this Theory harmonize the two, by showing that the Sun does *not* emanate Energy in *all* directions, equally, and at all times—but, on the contrary radiates Energy *only along the lines of Gravitation, and in proportion to the relative distances and sizes of the bodies to whom such Energy is radiated*?

The writer need scarcely state that in the short space at his disposal, in the pages of this book, he has been able merely to outline his Theory of Dynamic Force, as applied to the Inorganic World. The patience of the average reader has limits—and he must pass on to other features of the workings of the theory, namely the Mental Life of Man, in which the same laws are manifested. But, he feels that those interested in the phases of the subject touched upon, may explain for themselves the missing details by reference to the teachings of Modern Science on the subjects of Physics, remembering, *always*, to substitute the Theory of Dynamic Thought for the "Ether" theory that Modern Science borrows from Aristotle as a temporary "makeshift." The writer believes that this Theory will account for many of the missing links in Physics—a broad statement, he knows, and one either extremely impudent or superbly confident, according to the view-point of the critic.

The writer may be able to throw a little additional light, probably, upon the question of the relation between Gravitation, and the Excitement-waves of Radiant Energy. Without attempting to go into details, he wishes to suggest that in view of the fact that the Particles are connected by the "Lines of Gravitation," any great, extended, and rapid disturbance of a number of Particles would cause a series of undulating or wave-like movements in the "lines," which might be spoken of as waves of "Agitation or Unrest" in the Lines of Gravitation. This Agitation, or Unrest, of course, would be thus communicated to all other Particles toward whom lines extended, the intensity or effect of such Agitation or Unrest depending upon the relative distances, and the number of Particles involved. We may easily imagine how the intense and high rate of vibration among the Particles of the Sun, manifesting as intense Heat, would cause a like high degree of Agitation or Unrest among the Lines of Gravitation—the "lines" dancing backward and forward; around and about; following the movements of the Particles, and thus producing "waves" of Gravitational Agitation and Unrest, which when communicated to the Particles of the Earth, would produce a similar

Excitement among the Particles of the latter. In the same way the "Sun-spots," and consequent terrestial electrical disturbance may be explained.

While not absolutely tying himself to this particular conception of the details of the workings of the law, the writer feels free to say that he considers it a very reasonable idea, and one that in all probability will be found to come nearer to explaining the phenomena, than any other hypothesis. It certainly coincides with the "undulatory wave" theory of Science. The idea is but crudely expressed here, for lack of space, it being impossible to attempt to go into details—the mere mention of general principles being all that is possible at this time and place.

And now, for a few additional words on the subject of our theory that in place of the hypothetical Ether of Science—a Substance that is not Substance—there exists a great Ocean of Cosmic Mind. The idea is not without coroborative proof in the direction of the thought of advanced thinkers even among the ranks of Science.

While Science has accustomed the public to the idea that in the Universal Ether might be found the origin of Matter—the essence of Energy—the secret of Motion—it has not spoken of "Mind," in connection with this Universal Something. But the idea is not altogether new, and some daring Scientific thinkers have placed themselves on record regarding same. Let us quote from a few of them—it will make smoother our path.

Edward Drinker Cope, in several of his writings, hinted at the idea that *the basis of Life and Consciousness lay back of the Atoms, and might be found in the Universal Ether.*

Dolbear says: "Possibly the Ether may be the medium through which Mind and Matter react."

Hemstreet says: "Mind in the Ether is no more unnatural than Mind in flesh and blood."

Stockwell says: "The Ether is coming to be apprehended as an *immaterial*, superphysical substance, filling all space, carrying in its infinite throbbing bosom the specks of aggregated dynamic force called worlds. *It embodies the ultimate spiritual principle*, and represents the unity of those forces and energies from which spring, as their source, all phenomena, physical, *mental and spiritual*, as they are known to man."

Dolbear speaks of the Ether as a substance, which, besides the function of energy and motion, has other inherent properties "*out of which could emerge, under proper circumstances, other phenomena, such as life, or mind or whatever may be in the substratum.*"

Newton spoke of it as a "*subtle spirit, or immaterial substance.*" *Dolbear* says: "The Ether—the properties of which *we vainly strive to interpret in the terms of Matter*, the undiscovered properties of which ought to warn every one against the danger of strongly asserting what is possible and what is impossible in the nature of things."

Stockwell says: "That the Ether *is not Matter in any of its forms*, practically all scientists are agreed. *Dolbear*, again, says: If the Ether that fills all space is not atomic in structure, presents no friction to bodies moving through it, and is not subject to the law of gravitation, it *does not seem proper to call it Matter*. One might speak of it as a substance if he wants another name for it. As for myself, I make *a sharp distinction between the Ether and Matter*, and feel somewhat confused to hear one speak of the Ether as Matter."

And yet, in spite of the above expressions, no Scientist has dared to say in plain words that the Ether, or whatever took the place of the Ether, *must be Mind*, although several seem to be on the verge of the declaration, but apparently afraid to voice their thought.

In view of what we have seen in our consideration of the facts and principles advanced in this chapter, we are invited to consider the following two Supplemental Propositions:

SUPPLEMENTAL PROPOSITION III.—*Connecting each Particle of Substance with each and every other Particle of Substance, there exists "lines" of Mental Connection, the "thickness" of which depends upon the distance between the two particles, decreasing in proportion as the distance is increased. These "lines" may be considered as "conditions" of the great Ocean of Cosmic Mind which pervades and fills all Space, including the essence or inner being of the Particles of Substance, as well as the space between the said Particles. These "lines" are the "Lines of Gravitation," by and over which the phenomenon of Gravitation is manifested. These Lines of Gravitation have always existed between each Particle and every other Particle, and have persisted continuously and constantly, throughout all the changes of condition, and position, and relation, that the Particles have undergone. There is no "passage" or "transmission" of Energy or Force of Gravitation over these lines, or any other channel, but, on the contrary the Energy or Force of Gravitation is a constant and continuous Mental Connection or Bond existing between the Mind of the Particles, rather than between their Substance or Material.*

SUPPLEMENTAL PROPOSITION IV.—*The Lines of Gravitation, mentioned in the preceding proposition, are the medium over which travel, or are transmitted the "Thought-waves" resulting from the Excitement of the Particles, and by which waves the "Mental States" are communicated or transmitted. The same medium transmits or carries the Mental Force of Attraction—Cohesion, Chemical Affinity, etc., evidencing in the relation of the Particles to each other. Thus Gravitation not only performs its own work, but also acts as a "common carrier" for the "waves of Excitement," manifesting as Radiant Energy; and the waves of Desire-Force, manifesting as Attractive Energy.*

And here, the writer rests his case in the action in the Forum of Advanced Thought, entitled "*The Theory of Dynamic Thought vs. The Theory of Aristotle's Ether*," in which he appears for the Plaintiff. He begs that you, the members of the jury, will give to the evidence, and argument, due consideration, to the end that you may render a just verdict.

CHAPTER-XIV
The Mystery of Mind

THE writer, in this book, has treated the two manifestations of Life, *viz.*, Mind and Substance, as if they were separate things, although he has hinted at his belief that Substance, at the last, might be found to emanate from Mind, and be but a cruder form of its expression. The better way to express the thought would be to say that he believes that both Substance, and Mind *as we know it*, are but expressions of a form of Mind as much higher than *that which we know as Mind*, as the latter is higher than Substance. But he does not intend to follow up this belief, in this book, as the field of the work lies along other lines. The idea is mentioned here, merely for the purpose of giving a clew to those who might be interested in the conclusions of the writer, regarding this more remote regions of the general subject.

The writer agrees with the Ancient Occult Teachings regarding the existence of The Cosmic Mind, as he has stated in the last chapter. This Cosmic Mind, he believes, is independent of Substance, in fact it is the Mother of Substance, and its twin-brother, *Mind as we know it.*

Mind, as we know it, and Substance are always found in connection with other. It is true that the form of Substance, used by Mind as its body, may be far finer than the rarest vapor that we know, but it is Substance nevertheless. The working of the Great Plan of the Universe seems to require that Mind shall always have a body with which to work, and this rule applies not only in the case of the densest form of Substance and the Mind-principle manifesting through it, but also in the case of the highest manifestation of Mind, as we know it, which requires a body through which to manifest.

This constant combination of Mind and Substance—the fact that no Substance has been found without at least a trace of Mind, and no Mind except in relation to and combination with Substance, has led many scientific thinkers to accept the Materialistic idea that Mind was but a property of Substance, or a quality thereof. Of course, these philosophers and thinkers have had to admit that they could form no idea of the real nature of Mind, and could not conceive how Substance really *could* "think," but they found the Materialistic idea a simpler one that its opposite, and so they fell into it. Notwithstanding the fact that there was always a Something Within that would cry "Pshaw!" at the conclusion of the argument or illustration, these men have thought it reasonable to believe that there was no such thing as Mind, except as a result of "irritation of tissue," etc. But, nevertheless, there is always a Something in us that, in spite of argument, keeps crying like a child, "*'taint so*!" And, wonderful to relate, we heed the little voice.

This Materialistic theory is a curious reversal of the facts of the case. Even the very conclusions and reasoning of these thinkers is made possible only by the existence of that Mind which they would deny. The human reason is incapable of "explaining" the inner operation of the Mind, upon a strictly and purely physical basis. *Tyndall,* the great English scientist, truthfully said, *"the passage from the physics of the brain, to the corresponding facts of consciousness, is unthinkable. Granted that a definite thought and a definite molecular action of the brain occur simultaneously, we do not possess the intellectual organ, nor apparently any rudiment of the organ, which would enable us to pass by a process of reasoning from the one phenomenon to the other."*

The Materialist is prone to an attempt to rout the advocates of "Mind" with a demand for an answer to the question, "What is Mind?" The best answer to that question lies along the proverbial Irishman's lines of answering a question by asking another one, resulting in the "answering question," "What is *Matter*?" As a fact, the human reason is unable to give an intelligent answer to either question, and the best opinion seems to be to consider them as but two aspects of Something, the real origin of which lies in Something Higher, of which both are aspects or forms of expression.

The Occult Teaching, with which the writer agrees, is that the "Mind" inherent in any portion of substance, from the Corpuscle up to the Brain of Man, is but a segregated (or apparently separated) portion of the Universal Mind-principle, or Cosmic Mind. This fragment of Mind is always connected with Substance, and, in fact, it is believed that it is separated from the Universal Mind, and the other Separate Minds by a "film" of the rarest Substance, so fine as to be scarcely distinguishable from Mind. This separation is not a total separation, however, for the fragment of Mind is in connection with all other fragments of Mind, by "mental filaments," and besides is never out of touch with the Cosmic Mind.

But, comparatively, the fragment of Mind is *apart* from the rest, and we must consider it in this way, at least for the purpose of study, consideration, and illustration. It is like a drop in the Ocean of Mind, although connected, in a way, with every other drop, and the Ocean itself.

The individual Mind is not closely confined within the Substance in which it abides, but extends beyond the physical limits of the Substance, sometimes to a quite considerable distance. The Aura, or egg-shaped projection or emanation of Mind, surrounding each Particle and each Individual, is an instance of this. In addition to the Aura, there is possibly an extension of Mind to a considerable distance beyond the immediate vicinity of the physical limits, the connection, however, never being broken during the "life" term.

Mental influence at a distance, however, does not always require the above mentioned projection of the Mind. Thought-waves often answer the purpose, and, besides, there is such a thing as the imparting of Mental vibrations to the small particles of Substances with which the atmosphere is filled, which vibrations continue for quite a time, often for a long period after the presence of the individual producing them. These matters shall be discussed in later chapters of this book.

The Mind of Man is a far more complex thing that is generally imagined by the average man. Not only in its varied manifestation of consciousness, but its great region of "below-consciousness" or Infra Consciousness, as it is called. It shall be the purpose of the sequel to this book (now in preparation) which will be entitled "The Wonders of the Mind," to describe these inner workings, and to point out methods of utilizing the same.

Our next chapter, entitled "The Finer Forces of the Mind," will lead us into this field.

CHAPTER-XV
The Finer Forces of The Mind

IT was the writer's original intention to close the book with the chapter in which he brought to a close his argument, and presentation of the case of "Dynamic Thought." The book was written for the purpose of demonstrating that Theory, and it naturally should have closed there. The writer has in simultaneous course of preparation a companion book, entitled "*The Wonders of The Mind*," in which, in addition to information and instruction regarding the latent powers and hidden regions of the mind—including an investigation of the Infra-conscious and Ultra-conscious Regions; Automatic Thinking; Occult Systems of Mentation; Mental Development, and Unfoldment, etc.—he purposes taking up the subject of "Dynamic Thought," from the Mental Plane of Man. And he thought it better to keep the two branches of the subject separate and apart.

But, notwithstanding the above facts, he feels that he cannot close the present book—the consideration of the present phase of the subject, without at least a passing reference to the fact that "Dynamic Thought" is fully operative on the Plane of Human Mentation, as on the Plane of Atomic Mentation. In fact, Man has the same power, potentially, that is possessed by the Atom, only refined to a degree corresponding to the development of Man as compared to that of the Atom. The Power is raised to a higher Plane of Mentation, but is fully operative.

Just as the body of Man contains physical life corresponding with the different stages of lower physical life, mineral, vegetable, and animal—for instance, the mineral-like bones, and the mineral salts in the system; the plant-like life and work of the cells; and the animal-like flesh, and physical life; in addition to the wonderful brain-structure and fine brain development, peculiar to Man—so has Man the lower Mental Qualities of the lower life, in addition to his glorious Human Consciousness that is reserved for the Highest Form of Life on the globe.

In his Mental regions, man has the power of the Atom of attracting particles of Substance to him, that he may combine it with other Substances in building up his body—then he has the plant-like cell mentation, that does the building-up work, and repairs wounds, and damaged parts, etc.—then he has the animal mentation evidencing in the passions, desires, and emotions of the purely animal nature, and which mentation, by the way, keeps Man busy in controlling by means of his higher mental faculties, that are God's gift to Man, and are not possessed by the animals. But all this will form part of the sequel, "*The Wonders of The Mind*," and are merely mentioned here in passing.

And, just as Man is enabled to use elementary the physical qualities that he finds in his body, and to turn same to good account in living his human life, so does man, consciously, or unconsciously, make use of these elementary Mental powers in his everyday mental life. And if he but realizes what a *conscious* use of these faculties, guided by the Human Will, will do, Man may become a different order of being. This is the basis of the Occult Teachings, and the Mysteries of the Ancients, as well as the teachings of the modern secret esoteric bodies and societies, such as the "Rosicrucians" and "Hermetic Brotherhood," and several other societies whose names are not known—the *real* societies are referred to, not the brazen imitations that unscrupulous men are holding out to the public as the original orders, membership being offered and urged for the consideration of a few dollars. It is needless to say that membership in the *real* Occult orders is *never urged*, and *cannot be bought*.

But to return to the subject—the Individual Mind of Man is in direct touch, not only with the great Cosmic Mind, but also with the Individual Mind of every other Man. Just as the Particles are bound by lines of Attraction, so are the Minds of Men bound together by lines of Mind, or Mental filaments. And just as special forms of Attraction exist between the Particles, so do special forms of Attraction exist between Men. And just as Particles are influenced at a distance by other Particles, so are Men influenced at a distance by other Men. And just as the Particle draws toward itself that which it Desires, so do Men draw toward themselves that which they Desire. And just as Mental-States and "Excitement" are transmitted, or communicated from Particle to Particle, so are Mental States or "Excitement" transmitted or communicated from Men to Men. "*As Above so Below—as Below so Above*," says the old Occult Maxim, and it may be found to operate on every plane.

The phenomena of Thought Transference; Telepathy; Telesthesia; Mental Projection; Suggestion; Hypnotism, Mesmerism, etc., etc., may be explained and understood, by reason of an acquaintance with the "Theory of Dynamic Thought," as explained in this book. An understanding of one gives you the key to the other—for the Law operates precisely the same on each particular plane. If the reader will think over this statement, and then apply it to his investigations and experiments, he will find that he has the key to many mysteries—the loose end of a mighty ball of thread, which he may unwind at his leisure.

Let us begin by a consideration of the process of Thought-production in the Human Mind. In this way we may arrive at a clearer idea of the Mental Phenomena known as Thought-Force; Mental Power; Thought-waves; Thought-vibrations; Mind-transference; Mental Influence, etc. To understand these things we must begin by understanding the Process of Thought-production. Here is found the Secret of the phenomena named, and much more.

In the first place, while the Brain is the Organ of the Mind—the Instrument that the Mind uses in producing Thought, still the Brain does *not* do the thinking, nor is the brain-matter visible to the eye, the material instrument of thinking. The Brain (and other portions of the nervous systems, including the "little brains" or ganglia, found in various parts of the body) is composed of a certain substance—a fine form of Plasm, which however is but the ground-work of foundation for finer forms of Substance used in the production of Thought. Science has not discovered this finer Substance, for it is not visible to the eye, or to the finest instruments, but trained Occulists know that it exists. This fine Substance escapes the scalpel and microscope of the biologists and anatomists, and, consequently, their search for "Mind" in the Brain is futile. There is something more than "tissue to be irritated" in the Brain. But, remember, that this "something more" is still Substance, and not Mind itself.

Thought is a form of "Excitement" in this fine brain-substance, which we may as well call Psycho-plasm, from the two Greek words meaning "the mind," and "a mold, or matrix," respectively—the combined word meaning the "mould or matrix of Mind," in other words the material Substance used by the Mind in which to "cast" or "mold" Thoughts.

This Excitement in the Psychoplasm manifests in vibrations of its particles—for, like all Substance, it has "particles." All scientists agree that in the process of thinking there is an expenditure of Energy, and a "using-up" of material Substance. Just how this is effected, they do not know, but their experiments have shown that there is Energy manifested and used, and also Substance consumed.

The secret of the production of Thought does not lie in the Brain or nervous system, which are but the material substratum upon which the Mind works, and which it uses as a mold or matrix for the production of Thought. Thought is the product of Mind directing Force upon Substance in the shape of Psychoplasm. And Energy is manifested in the production of Thought just as much as in the operation of the Law of Attraction, or Chemical Action. "*What* Force and Energy?" may be asked. The answer is "*Mental* Force!" But although the answer stares them right in the face, scientists deny that Mind contains Force or Energy within itself, and persist in thinking of Force as a "mechanical thing," or as necessarily derived from the common forms of Energy, such as Heat, Light or Electricity. They ignore the fact that Mind has a Finer Force which it uses to perform its work.

How do the Atoms attract each other and move together? There is an evidence of Force and Energy here that is not Heat, Light or Electricity—what is it? When a man wishes to close his hand, he Wills that it be closed, and sends a current of this Finer Force of the Mind along the nerve to the muscle, and the latter contracts and the hand is closed. A similar process is used in every muscular action. *What is the Force used?*

Science admits the existence of this Force, and calls it "Nervous Energy," or "Nerve Force." It holds that it must be something like Electricity, and some even go so far as to say that it *is* Electricity. They base their ideas upon the fact that when Electricity is applied to the muscle of living or dead animals, they contract just as they do when this "Nerve Force" is applied, and every movement of the muscles may be so produced by Electricity, which becomes a counterfeit Nerve Force. But, here is the point, this Force cannot be identical with Electricity, *for none of the appliances for registering electric currents will register it*. It is not Electricity, *but is some Finer Force of the Mind*, generated in the material substratum that the Mind uses as a base of operation.

This Fine Force of the Mind is generated in some way in the Brain and Nervous System, by action upon the Psychoplasm. The Brain, or brains (for Man has several centres worthy of that term) are like great dynamos and storehouses of this Force, and the nerves are the wires that carry it to all parts of the system. More than this, the nerves have been found to be generators of Force, also, as well as the Brain. Experiments have shown that the supply of Force in a nerve vanishes when the nerve is used, in which case it draws upon the storehouses for an additional supply.

This Fine Force of the Mind is really the source of All Energy, for as we have shown in previous chapters, all Motion arises from Mental Action, and this form of Force or Energy is the primal Force or Energy produced by the Mind. And this Force is in operation in all forms of Life, from the Atom to the Man. And not only may it be used by the Particle, but Man, also, has it at his disposal.

As a proof that Substance is "used-up," and Energy manifested in the production of Thought, Science points to the fact that the temperature of a nerve rises when it is used, and the temperature of the Brain increases when it is used for extended Thought. Scientists have claimed, and advanced a mass of proof to back up the same, that Thought was as much a form of Energy as was the pulling of a train of cars, and was attended by the production of a definite amount of Heat, resulting from the activity of the fine substance of the physical extended resistant and composite substratum.

But, Science has taken all this to mean that Thought and Mind were purely material things, and properties of Matter. It has claimed that "Matter Thinks," instead of that Mind uses the Matter or Substance, in its finer forms, as a *substratum for the production of Thought*. Buchner, the leader of the purely Materialistic school, claims positively that Thought is but the product of Matter. He says: "Is it not a patent fact, obvious to all but the wilfully blind that *matter does think*? De la Mettrie made merry over the narrowness of the mentalists, in saying: 'When people ask whether matter can think, it is as though they asked whether matter can strike the hours!' Matter, indeed, as such, thinks as little as it strikes the hours; but it does both, when brought into such conditions that thinking, or hour-striking results as a natural action or performance."

The above quoted opinion of Buchner shows how narrow and one-sided a talented man may become by reason of shutting out all other points of view, and seeing only one phase of a subject. The example of the "hour-striking" is a poor figure for the Materialists, for although matter *does* strike the hours, it does so only when wound up by Man under direction of his Mind. And in the manufacture, adjustment, and winding of the clock, Mind is the Cause of the Action. And, more than this, the very action of the coiled spring that is the immediate cause of the striking, results from the *mental* effort of the Particles of the spring endeavoring to resume their accustomed position, under the law of Elasticity, as explained in our chapters on Substance.

Science renders valuable service in showing us the details of the "mechanism" of Thought, but it will never really *explain* anything unless it assumes the existence of Mind, back of and in everything. It may dissect the brain-cells, and show us their composition, but it never will find Mind under the scalpel, or in the scale or test-tube. Not only is this true, but it cannot even discover the fine Psychoplasm which is used in the production of Mind. But we may make use of its investigations regarding the matter of Activity of Brain-substance in the process of Thought, and by combining them with our belief regarding the existence of Mind we may form a complete chain of reasoning, without any missing-links—these missing-links appearing both in the case of the "no-mind" philosophers, and the "no-matter" metaphysicians.

This theory of Mind and Substance considered as the two aspects of Something Higher, from which both have originated or emanated, will come to be regarded as the only "thinkable" proposition, in the end. And, with this idea in view, we may use the facts and experiments of the Materialists, while smiling at their theories. And, with but a slight change of words, we may turn against them their own verbal batteries. In this way, we may take Moleschott's famous statement: "*Thought is but a motion of Matter*," and render it intelligible by making it read as follows: "*Thought produces Motion in Matter*."

This Finer Force of the Mind is in full evidence to those who look for it, and although it may not be registered by the scales or instruments designed to register the coarser grades of Force, still it *is* registered in the minds of men and women, and in the actions resulting from their thoughts. These living registers of the Force respond readily to it,—and every one of us is such a register. Just as is the Force a much higher grade of Energy than the forms usually considered as comprising the entire range of Energy, so are the instruments required for its registration much higher than those used to determine the degrees of Heat, Light, Electricity, and Magnetism. It may be that the future will give us instruments adapted for the purpose—in fact it begins to look even now as if the same were forthcoming. But whether we have such mechanical instruments, or not, the living instruments give us a sufficient proof of the existence of the Force, and its operation.

Well—the writer still finds himself unable to bring the book to a close. He added this chapter, to show that the property of Dynamic Thought extended to the highest development of Mind, as well as abiding in the lowest. And, now that he has ventured upon the subject, he finds himself impelled to give you a few instances of the workings and operations of that Law, in the case of Human Mental Life. And this means one more chapter—but only one, remember. The book must come to an end sometime remember. And, so we will pass over into another chapter, which will be entitled, "Thought in Action."

CHAPTER-XVI

Thought In Action

WITHOUT attempting to go into details, or to enter into explanations, the writer purposes taking his readers on a flying trip through the region of "Thought in Action," or "Dynamic Thought in Operation in Human Life." The details of this fascinating region must be left for another and more extended visit, in our next book (before mentioned) which will be called "*The Wonders of The Mind.*" But he thinks that even this flying trip will prove of interest and instruction.

Let us start with a hasty look at Man himself. Not to speak of his "Seven Planes of Mind," which belongs to the next visit, we find him a very interesting object. Not only has he a physical body, apparent to our senses, but he has also a finer or "astral body," which he may use (unconsciously, or consciously, when he learns how) for little excursions away from the body, during his lifetime. This Astral Body is composed of Substance just as his denser physical body. The field and range of Substance extends far beyond the powers of ordinary vision, as even the Materialists must admit when they talk of "Radiant Matter," "Etherial Substance," etc. Then he has currents of Fine Force coursing through his nervous system, which may be seen by those possessing "Astral Vision," if the teachings of the Occultists be true.

Then he, like the Particle, has an "Aura" or egg-shaped projection of Mind and fine particles of Psychoplasm, which has been thrown off in the process of Thought, and which clusters around him, producing a "Mental Atmosphere," which constantly surrounds him, and makes itself "felt" by those coming in his presence. Those who read these words may remember, readily, the "feeling" they have experienced when coming in contact with certain people—how some radiated an atmosphere of cheerfulness, brightness, etc., while others radiated the very opposite. Some radiate a feeling of energy, activity, etc., while others manifest just the reverse. Many likes and dislikes between people meeting for the first time, arise in this way, each finding in the mental atmosphere of the other, some inharmonious element. These radiations are perceived by others coming into their range.

Occultists tell us that the character of a man's thought vibrations may be determined by certain colors, which are visible to those having "Astral Sight." There is nothing so wonderful about this, when it is remembered that the various "colors" of light, comprising the visible colors of the spectrum, ranging from red, on through orange, yellow, green, blue, indigo, and terminating in violet, arise simply from different rates of vibration of the Particles of Substance. And as Thought is produced by Mind causing vibrations in the Psychoplasm, why is not the Astral Colors reasonable? We cannot stop to consider these colors in detail, but may run over the ones corresponding to each marked Emotion of Thought, as reported by the Occult teachings.

For instance the shade of the thought manifesting in physical or organic functions, is of a colorless white, or "color of clear water"; and the color of the thought manifesting in Fine Force or Vital Energy, is that of air,—heated air arising from a furnace or heated ground—when it emerges from the body although of a faint pink when in the body itself. Black represents Hate, Malice, etc.; Gray (bright shade) represents Selfishness, while Gray of a dark dull shade represents Fear. Green represents Jealousy, Deceit, Treachery, and similar emotions, ranging from the dull shades which characterize the lower and cruder forms, to the bright shades which characterize the finer, or more delicate forms of "Tact," "Politeness," "Diplomacy," etc. Red (dull shade) represents Sensuality and Animal Passion, while red (bright and vivid) represents Anger. Crimson, in varying shades, represents the phases of "Love." Brown represents Avarice or Greed. Orange represents Pride and Ambition; and Yellow, in varying shades, represents grades of Intellectual Power. Blue is the color of the Religious thoughts, ranging, however, through a great variety of stages, from the dull shade of superstitious religious belief, to the beautiful violet of the highest religious emotion or thought. What is generally known as "Spirituality" is characterized by a Light Blue of a peculiarly luminous shade. Just as there are ultra-red, and ultra-violet rays in the spectrum, which the eye cannot perceive, so Occultists inform us there are "colors" in the Aura or Mental Atmosphere of a person of unusual psychic or occult development, the ultra-violet rays indicating the thought of one who is pursuing the higher planes of occult thought and unfoldment, while the ultra-red is evidenced by those possessing occult development, but who are using the same for base and selfish purposes—"black-magic" in fact. There are other shades, known to Occultists, indicating several highly developed states of Mind, but it is needless to mention them here.

But the influence of these Particles of "Thought-stuff" thrown off from the Mind Psychoplasm under the vibrations produced by the Mind during the process of Thought, does not cease with the phenomena surrounding the Aura. They are radiated to a considerable distance, and produce a number of effects. We will remember how the Corpuscles or Electrons are thrown off by Substance in a high state of vibration. Well, the same law manifests in the vibrations attendant upon the production of Thought. The particles are thrown off in great quantities each vibrating at the rate imparted to it during the process. No these particles of "Thought-stuff" do not compose the "Thought-waves"—the latter belong to a different set of phenomena.

These particles of vibrating "Thought-stuff" fly off from the brain of the thinker, in all directions, and affect other persons who may come in contact with them. There is an important rule here, however, and that is that they seem to be attracted by those minds which are vibrating in similar thought-rates with themselves, and are but feebly attracted—and in some cases, actually repelled—by minds vibrating on opposite lines of Thought. "Like attracts Like," in the Thought World, and "Birds of a feather flock together," here as elsewhere.

Some of these particles of "Thought-stuff" are still in existence, and vibrating, which proceeded from the minds of persons long since dead, the same being emitted or thrown off during the lifetime of the persons, however. Just as a distant star, which was destroyed hundreds of years ago, may have emitted rays which are only now reaching our vision, years after the destruction of the star which emitted them—and just as an odor will remain in a room after the object causing it has departed the particles still remaining and vibrating—and just as a stove removed from a room may leave heat vibrations behind it—so do these particles persist, vibrate, and influence other minds, long after the person who caused them may have passed out of the body. In this way, rooms, houses, neighborhoods, and localities may vibrate with the thoughts of people who lived there long ago, but who have since passed away, or removed. These vibrations affect people living in these places, to a greater or lesser extent, depending upon circumstances, but they may always be counteracted or changed (if they are of undesirable nature) by setting upon positive vibrations on a different plane of mind, or character of thought.

The mind of a thinker is constantly emitting or throwing off these particles of "Thought-stuff"; the distance and rate of speed, to and by which they travel, being determined by the "force" used in their production, there being a great difference between the thought of a vigorous thinker, and that emanating from a weak, listless mind. These projections of Thought-stuff have a tendency to mingle with others of a corresponding rate of vibration (depending upon the character of the thought.) Some remain around the places where they were emitted, while others float off like clouds, and obey the Law of Attraction which draws them to persons thinking along similar lines.

The characteristics of cities arise in this way, the general average of Thought of their inhabitants causing a corresponding Thought-atmosphere to hang over and around it, which atmosphere is distinctly felt by visitors, and often determines the mental character of the persons residing there, in spite of their previous characteristics—*that is, unless they understand the Laws of Thought*. Some neighborhoods, also, have their own peculiar Mental Atmosphere, as all may have noticed if they have visited certain "tough" neighborhoods, on the one hand, and neighborhoods of an opposite kind, on the other. Certain kinds of Thoughts and Actions seem to be contagious in certain places—*and they are* to those who do not understand the Law. Certain shops seem to have their own atmosphere—some reflecting confidence and honest dealing, and others radiating an atmosphere that causes patrons to hold tightly to their pocketbooks, and, in some extreme cases, to be certain that their buttons are tightly sewed on their garments. Yes, places like people, have their distinctive Mental Atmospheres, and both arise from the same cause.

And each person draws to himself these particles of vibrating "Thought-stuff" corresponding with the general mental attitude maintained by him. If one harbors feelings of Malice, he will find thoughts of malice, revenge, hate, etc., pouring in upon him. He has made himself a centre of Attraction, and has set the Law into operation. His only safe course is to resolutely change his thought vibrations.

A most remarkable form of these particles of Thought-stuff is evidenced in the case of what are known among occultists as "Thought-forms," which are aggregations of Particles of Thought-stuff energized by intense and positive thought, and which are sent out with such intensity and positiveness, that they are almost "vitalized," and manifest almost the same degree of mental influence that would be manifested by the sender if he were present where they are. This highly interesting phase of the subject would take many chapters to describe in detail, and we must content ourselves with a mere passing view. To those who are interested in the subject, the writer would say that he purposes considering them at considerable length, in the forthcoming book "*The Wonders of The Mind*," which has been alluded to elsewhere.

Besides the operation of these particles of Thought-stuff emitted during the production of Thought, there are many other phases of Thought Influence, or Thought in Action. The principal phase of this phenomena arises from the working of the Law of Attraction between the respective minds of different people. Just as are the Particles of Substance united and connected by "lines" of connection, so are the minds of Men connected. And the strong "pull" of Desire manifests along these lines, just as it does in the case of the Atoms. There has been much written of recent years regarding this "Drawing Power of the Mind," and although some of what has been written is the veriest rubbish and nonsense, yet under it all there remains a strong, form, substantial substratum of Fact and Truth. Men *do* attract Success and Failure to them—people *do* attract things to them—as strange as it may seem to the person who has not acquainted himself with the laws underlying the phenomenon.

There is no "miracle" about all of this—it is simply that the Law of Attraction is in full operation, and that people of similar thoughts are drawn together by reason thereof. The workings of this Law are somewhat intricate, but all of us are constantly using them, consciously or unconsciously. We draw to ourselves that which we Desire very much, or that which we Fear very much, for a Fear is a Belief, and acts in the direction of actualizing itself, *sometimes*. But, again, as Kipling would say: "But, that's another story." This phase of the subject is a mighty subject in itself, and "the half has not been told" even by the many who have written of it. The writer intends to try to remedy the deficiency in his next book, however.

Then, again, the "Excitement" of Thought, in the minds of people may be transmitted or communicated to the minds of others, and a similar vibration set up, under certain conditions, and subject to certain restraining influences—just as in the case of the Particles of Substances in a body or Mass of Substance. And, in many ways that will suggest themselves to the reader who has mastered the contents of the earlier chapters of this book, the phenomena of Dynamic Thought in the case of the Atoms, and Particles, may be, and are duplicated in the case of Individual Minds of Men.

The reader will see, readily, that this theory of Dynamic Thought, and the facts noted in the consideration thereof, give an intelligent explanation for the respective phenomena of Hypnotism, Mesmerism, Suggestion, Thought-transference, Telepathy, etc., as well as of Mental Healing, Magnetic Healing, etc., all of which are manifestations of "Dynamic Thought." Not only do we see, as Prentice Mulford said, that "Thoughts are Things," but we may see "*just why*" they are Things. And we may see and understand the laws of their production and operation. This theory of Dynamic Thought will throw light into many dark corners, and make plain many "hard sayings" that have perplexed you in the past. The writer believes that it gives us the key to many of the great Riddles of Life.

This theory has come to stay. It is no ephemeral thing, doomed to "die a-borning." It will be taken up by others and polished, and added to, and shaped, and "decorated"—but the fundamental principles will stand the stress of Time and Men. Of this the writer feels assured. It may be laughed at at first, not only by the "man on the street," but also by the scientists. But it will outlive this, and in time will come to its own—perhaps long after the writer and the book have been forgotten.

This must be so—for the idea of "Dynamic Thought" underlies the entire Universe, and is the cause of all phenomena. Not only is all that we see as Life and Mind, and Substance illustrations of the Law, but even that which lies back of these things must evidence the same Law. Is it too daring a conception to hazard the thought that perhaps the Universe itself is *the result of the Dynamic Thought of The Infinite*?

Oh, Dynamic Thought, we see in thee the instrument by which all Form and Shape are created, changed and destroyed—we see in thee the source of all Energy, Force and Motion—we see thee Always—present and Everywhere—present, and always in Action. Verily, thou art Life in Action. Thou art the embodiment of Action and Motion, of which Zittel hath said: "Wherever our eyes dwell on the Universe; whithersoever we are carried in the flight of thought, everywhere we find Motion." Suns, planets, worlds, bodies, atoms, and particles, move, and act at thy bidding. Amidst all the change of Substance—among the play of Forces—and among and amidst all that results therefrom—there art thou, unchanged, and constant. As though fresh from the hand of The Infinite, thou hast maintained thy vigor and strength, and power, throughout the aeons of Time. And, likewise, Space has no terrors for thee, for thou hath mastered it. Thou art a symbol of the Power of The Infinite—thou art Its message to doubting Man!

Let us close this book with the thought of the Greatness of this Thing that we call Dynamic Thought—which, great as it is, is but as the shadow of the Absolute Power of The Infinite One, which is the Causeless Cause, and the Causer of Causes. And in thus parting company, reader, let us murmur the words of the German poet, who has sung:

> "Dost thou ask for rest? See then how foolish is thy desire; the stern yoke of motion holds in harness the whole Universe.
>
> "Nowhere in this age canst thou ever find rest, and no power can deliver thee from the doom of Activity.
>
> "Rest is not to be found either in heaven or on earth, and from death and dying break forth new growth,—new birth.
>
> "All the life of Nature is an ocean of Activity; following on her footsteps, without ceasing, thou must march forward with the whole.
>
> "Even the dark portal of death gives thee no rest, and out of thy coffin will spring blossoms of a new life."

FINIS

www.ingramcontent.com/pod-product-compliance
Ingram Content Group UK Ltd.
Pitfield, Milton Keynes, MK11 3LW, UK
UKHW040318300826
14791UKWH00003B/973

9 789355 840141